THE JOY OF BRIDGE™ COMPANION

THE JOY OF BRIDGE™ COMPANION

Audrey Grant
and
Eric Rodwell

Prentice-Hall Canada Inc. Scarborough, Ontario

Canadian Cataloguing in Publication Data

Grant, Audrey.
   The joy of bridge companion

Supplement to: Grant, Audrey. The joy of bridge.
ISBN 0-13-511502-7

1. Contract bridge - Problems, exercises, etc.
I. Rodwell, Eric. II. Grant, Audrey. The joy
of bridge. III. Title.

GV1282.3.G732 1986   795.41'5   C86-093545-0

Prentice-Hall, Inc., Englewood Cliffs, New Jersey
Prentice-Hall International, Inc., London
Prentice-Hall of Australia, Pty., Sydney
Prentice-Hall of India Pvt., Ltd., New Delhi
Prentice-Hall of Japan, Inc., Tokyo
Prentice-Hall of Southeast Asia (Pte.) Ltd., Singapore
Editora Prentice-Hall do Brasil Ltda., Rio de Janeiro
Prentice-Hall Hispanoamericana, S.A., Mexico
Whitehall Books Limited, Wellington, New Zealand

ISBN 0-13-511502-7

Production Editor: Kathleen Niccols
Cover Design: Gail Ferreira-Ng-A-Kien
Production: Joanne Matthews

Printed and bound in Canada by Webcom Limited
1 2 3 4 5 W 90 89 88 87 86

TABLE OF CONTENTS

INTRODUCTION

Learning to play bridge is a continual evolution; you read, play, observe, draw conclusions and repeat the whole process. The game, like so many other dynamic things in life, has the potential to be a fascination or a frustration. It all depends on your attitude. You have to be patient and curious. You have to be comfortable with more questions than answers.

The Joy of Bridge provides one of the best ways to learn bridge or to upgrade your game. If you are learning with friends and relatives, or with a bridge teacher, the exercises in *The Companion* provide a great way to put theory into practice. Each unit corresponds to a chapter in the text.

Preparation

Before trying the exercises, become familiar with the material in the corresponding chapter of *The Joy of Bridge*. You might try getting your group together and reading the chapter aloud. It is a pleasant way to spend time. Oral reading and listening are almost forgotten pleasures. If you are in a bridge class, the teacher can present the material.

Each exercise is designed for four players but will work with any number. If you have extra players, rotate them in at the end of each exercise. Everyone can join in the discussion of each hand. If you are learning individually, follow the exercises, deal out the hands and play all four hands yourself.

The Chairperson

When an exercise involves a discussion, it can be handled in two ways. The teacher can lead the group or the students can take turns being chairperson. The chairperson leads the group in completing the exercise, getting the group to reach a consensus where necessary and acting as spokesperson if there are several groups each reporting to a teacher. The chairperson could rotate with each exercise that involves discussion: North, East, South and then West.

Let's Experiment

In many exercises, you construct hands. You can do this any way you want but here is a suggestion. Each person takes one suit and selects the required cards from it. For example, if one of the hands requires the Ace, Eight, Seven, Six and Three of Spades, then the person with the Spade suit puts those cards face-up on the table as shown in the diagram on page 11 of the textbook. Each of the other players then places their cards face-up on the table to form a complete hand.

Bidding

The exercises in the first twelve units are designed for bidding without competition. After one partnership has opened the bidding, the other partnership should pass throughout the auction, even though a player may be tempted to compete. Competitive bidding starts with unit thirteen.

Recording Tricks

Keep the cards played to each trick in the manner described on page six of the textbook. You will then be able to look at the hand again after you have played it. This is the best way to learn. In some exercises, the same hand is used more than once, so save your hand until the next exercise.

When you are looking at a hand that has been played, turn it face-up and arrange the suits in rows as if it were the dummy. This makes it easier to look at two hands or all four hands at once.

Summaries

There are summaries at the end of each unit where the student can fill in the appropriate words. This is a good review; you learn by writing things out. There are also completed summaries in Appendix IV.

Bidding Analysis Chart

The Bidding Analysis Chart is used as the basis for discussing the bidding after the hand has been played. It can be found in Appendix II.

Play of the Hand

Read chapters 24, 25 and 26 in *The Joy of Bridge*. These chapters present a good way of thinking about the play of the hand. The best way to improve is to be curious. If you don't make enough tricks, turn all of the hands up when you have finished. Review Declarer's Four Questions to see if there was anything you could have done to make the hand.

Answers

Many exercises will be answered through the discussions or with the help of a teacher. The answers can be found in Appendix III. The information to be filled in on the summary cards is found by referencing the appropriate chapter in *The Joy of Bridge* or from the summaries in Appendix IV.

Timeframe

The material in *The Joy of Bridge* and in *The Joy of Bridge Companion* can be covered over a period of time in a variety of ways. Here is a suggested outline for a twelve-week course of lessons, each lasting from two to three hours:

Lessons 6 and 7 discuss play and defense. They can be introduced any time during the course that is convenient for the teacher and students. The course can easily be expanded to twenty lessons or reduced to ten.

Attitude

Be comfortable making mistakes! Some of the world's greatest discoveries came about because people had the courage to be wrong. Be experimental and curious. Rather than looking for one right answer - it often does not exist - look to see what happens when you try something.

Be patient. Almost everyone has heard of players who remember every card played. You might wonder what you are expected to remember. We all know people who can run a marathon but it shouldn't spoil our walk around the block. Remember as much as you can and work one step at a time.

While the recommended methods lead to the best result on the majority of hands, there will occasionally be hands on which the result will be less than perfect. The more you try to find methods that work in all cases, the further you move from the methods that work for most hands.

Above all, remember that bridge is a game, one that can bring you entertainment, new friends and good times with your old friends for the rest of your life. It will keep you mentally fit and improve your memory. With all this going for it, you're sure to enjoy your adventure with bridge, the world's most popular card game.

UNIT ONE: GETTING STARTED

Joy of Bridge reference: pages 2 - 14

EXERCISE ONE: TAKING TRICKS

The player sitting North is the dealer and deals out the cards face-down and clockwise until all the cards are dealt; each player will have thirteen cards. Each player picks up his cards and sorts them into suits.

The dealer leads any card by placing it face-up on the table.
The other players, clockwise in turn, put a card of the same suit on the table (follow suit). If a player has no card in the suit led, he may play (discard) a card of another suit.
These four cards are called a trick. The player contributing the highest card in the suit led wins the trick. The Ace is high followed by the King, Queen, Jack, Ten . . . down to the two.
The player winning the trick leads to the next trick.

Keep the card played to the trick in front of you. If you win the trick, turn your card face-down and place it vertically at the edge of the table in front of you. If you lose the trick, turn the card face-down and place it horizontally at the edge of the table in front of you. At the end of the hand, the table will look something like the diagram on page six of the textbook. Playing the cards in this fashion has the advantage that you can look at your hand again afterwards.

Try to take as many tricks as you can.

Turn your winners, the cards that are vertically placed in front of you, face-up. Did anyone have a small card that took a trick?

_____

Turn your losers, the cards that are horizontally placed in front of you, face-up. Did anyone have a high card that didn't take a trick?

_____

Why do small cards sometimes take tricks?

_____

Why do high cards sometimes not take tricks?

_____

EXERCISE TWO: HOW MANY TRICKS DO YOU HAVE?

The deal moves clockwise around the table, so this time East deals.
After sorting your cards into suits, write down the cards in each suit that you think will win tricks. For example, if you have the A K 9 8 2 in a suit, you might predict taking tricks with the A, K and one or two little cards. Don't let the other players see what you have predicted.

	SPADES	HEARTS	DIAMONDS	CLUBS	TOTAL TRICKS
PREDICTION					
RESULTS					

Play the hand and try to win as many tricks as you can.
Write down the cards with which you won tricks and compare them with your prediction. What cards took tricks that you didn't think would be winners? What cards didn't take tricks that you thought would be winners?

_____

How does the total number of tricks predicted by the group compare with the thirteen tricks available?

_____

Did you like playing to a trick first, in the middle, or last?

_____

EXERCISE THREE: BUILDING TRICKS

Suppose your hand contains the following cards:

♠ K Q J 10 9 8
♥ A 7 6
♦ A 4 3
♣ A

Which card would you lead? Why?

_____

How many tricks would you expect to take?

_____

EXERCISE FOUR: CHOOSING A LEAD

Which card would you lead on each of the following hands? Why?

1)
♠ K 9 8
♥ Q J 10 9
♦ A 4 3
♣ 7 6 2

Lead: _____

2)
♠ Q 7 6 3 2
♥ A Q 9 4
♦ J 7 3
♣ A

Lead: _____

3)
♠ J 7 3
♥ K Q 10 6 3
♦ A 7
♣ 9 7 3

Lead: _____

EXERCISE FIVE: WORKING WITH A PARTNER

South deals.

Again, estimate the number of tricks your hand might take.

	SPADES	HEARTS	DIAMONDS	CLUBS	TOTAL TRICKS
PREDICTION					

This time, you are going to work with the player sitting opposite you, your partner, and help each other take as many tricks as you can. Before playing the hand, each partnership estimates the total number of tricks it plans to take.

	YOUR TOTAL	PARTNER'S TOTAL	COMBINED TOTAL
PREDICTION			

Try to take as many combined tricks as you can. Remember, if your partner is winning the trick, play low (don't take your partner's King with your Ace). When your partner leads his long suit, help him build tricks by leading the same suit when you get a chance.

How did you enjoy playing with a partner?

_____

Did you manage to build tricks in the suit that your side led first?

_____

EXERCISE SIX: THE TRUMP SUIT

West deals.

This time, the Spade suit will be trump or wild.

Again, estimate the tricks which you think you can take. Combine the total with that of your partner to estimate the total number of tricks the partnership is trying to take.

	SPADES	HEARTS	DIAMONDS	CLUBS	TOTAL TRICKS
PREDICTION					

	YOUR TOTAL	PARTNER'S TOTAL	COMBINED TOTAL
PREDICTION			

Take as many tricks as you can, working with your partner.

What difference is there between playing without a trump suit (No Trump) and playing with a trump suit?

_____

EXERCISE SEVEN: DECIDING ON THE TRUMP SUIT

North deals. This exercise has three parts:

i) Each partnership works together to decide what suit the partnership would like as trump by talking across the table. Everyone may speak at once. Use adjectives and adverbs, but no numbers, to describe your hand to partner, telling which suit you would like to have as the trump suit. The conversation might sound like this:

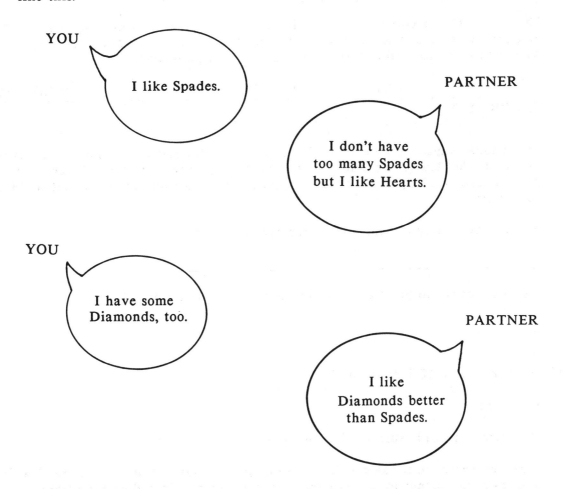

ii) Once the partnership reaches a consensus on the trump suit, it predicts the total number of tricks it could take with this suit as trump. The partnership willing to predict the higher number of tricks gets to name the trump suit. If there is a tie, flip a coin to decide for now.

iii) Now play the hand with the agreed suit as trump. The person who first mentioned the agreed trump suit is the declarer. The person on his left makes the opening lead. Declarer's partner is the dummy and puts his hand face-up on the table.

Pick up your hand and show it to your partner. Did you pick the longest combined suit as trump?

————

UNIT TWO: OPENING THE BIDDING AT THE ONE-LEVEL

Joy of Bridge reference: pages 15 - 25

Before play commences, the trump suit is determined through a process called bidding. Bridge bidding is like an auction. The privilege of naming the trump suit (or No Trump) goes to the highest bidder.

A player makes a bid by naming a level and a denomination (suit or No Trump). The level named includes an assumed six tricks (the book).

For example, a bid of One Club is a one-level bid naming Clubs as the denomination. It represents 6 + 1 = 7 tricks.

An opening bid describes to your partner something about the strength and the shape (distribution) of your hand.

EXERCISE ONE: THE BID

How many tricks do each of the following bids represent:

One Heart?   Two Spades?   Three No Trump?

_____   _____   _____

EXERCISE TWO: THE RANKING OF THE SUITS

Look at the Bidding Ladder.

Which is higher on the Bidding Ladder: One Spade or One No Trump?

_____

What is the lowest possible bid? What is the highest possible bid?

_____   _____

How many tricks does the lowest possible bid represent? How many tricks does the highest possible bid represent?

_____   _____

EXERCISE THREE: THE OPENING BID

The bidding starts with the dealer who makes an opening bid, suggesting a suit or No Trump, or passes the decision to the player on his left by saying "Pass."

What do you think are the most important factors in deciding whether or not to open the bidding?

_____

EXERCISE FOUR: BALANCED HANDS

A balanced hand is a hand that contains no voids, no singletons and at most one doubleton. Use the cards to construct as many balanced hands as you can. What hand patterns (shapes) could be considered as balanced?

_____   _____   _____

EXERCISE FIVE: OPENING THE BIDDING

Add up the High Card Points (HCP) and Length Points to determine the total number of points in each of the following hands:

1) ♠ A 9 7
   ♡ A 10 9
   ◇ A 4 3
   ♣ A J 4 2

   HCP: _____
   + Length Points: _____
   = Total Points: _____

2) ♠ K 6 5
   ♡ K 4 3
   ◇ K 9 8 7 3
   ♣ K J

   HCP: _____
   + Length Points: _____
   = Total Points: _____

3) ♠ A 8 7 3
   ♡ A K
   ◇ A 6 5
   ♣ A J 8 3

   HCP: _____
   + Length Points: _____
   = Total Points: _____

4) ♠ A K Q J
   ♡ 9 8 7 6 5 2
   ◇ K 7
   ♣ 2

   HCP: _____
   + Length Points: _____
   = Total Points: _____

5) ♠ Q
   ♡ K 8 7 4 3
   ◇ K 5 4 3 2
   ♣ A K

   HCP: _____
   + Length Points: _____
   = Total Points: _____

6) ♠ A 7 6 5
   ♡ A
   ◇ A J 4 3
   ♣ K Q 4 3

   HCP: _____
   + Length Points: _____
   = Total Points: _____

Circle the hands that are balanced.

EXERCISE SIX: OPENING ONE NO TRUMP

In Exercise Five, which hand would be opened One No Trump?

_____

Why would the other balanced hands not be opened One No Trump?

_____

Why would hand #5 not be opened One No Trump?

_____

EXERCISE SEVEN: OPENING BIDS AT THE ONE-LEVEL

Using the Summary Chart for Opening the Bidding (Appendix IV), decide what your opening bid would be on each of the hands in Exercise Five.

1) _____   2) _____   3) _____

4) _____   5) _____   6) _____

SUMMARY

HAND VALUE

HIGH CARD POINTS (HCPs)

Ace	____ Points
King	____ Points
Queen	____ Points
Jack	____ Point

LENGTH POINTS

5-Card Suit	____ Point
6-Card Suit	____ Points
7-Card Suit	____ Points
8-Card Suit	____ Points

OPENING THE BIDDING

With less than 13 points, _____.

With 13 to 21 points:

- Open the bidding _____ when you have 16 - 18 points and a balanced hand.

- Otherwise, open the bidding at the one-level in your

_____.

If you have a choice of suits:

- Bid the _____ of two five-card (or six-card) suits.

- Bid the _____ of two four-card suits.

- Bid the _____ of three four-card suits.

UNIT THREE: OBJECTIVES

Joy of Bridge reference: pages 26 - 33

You need to know how the scoring works so that you have a feeling for the objectives of the game. However, at this point, it is sufficient to understand that there are bonus levels for which extra points are awarded.

There are two common ways to keep score. One is the method used in *The Joy of Bridge*, which is similar to that used in tournament play. The other is Rubber Bridge scoring which is often used in informal games at home.

EXERCISE ONE: BONUS LEVELS

Mark the Game bonus levels on your Bidding Ladder (Appendix I).
Beside each bonus level, mark the trick score, the bonus and the total points scored for making Game.

Note: If you wish, you can omit the details of scoring in the following exercises until you have more experience with the game.

EXERCISE TWO: JOY OF BRIDGE SCORING PRACTICE (TOURNAMENT STYLE)

Assume you are playing a round of bridge (four hands). You and your partner are North-South and your opponents are East-West. Using the Scoring Summary in Appendix 3 of *The Joy of Bridge*, record the score on the score sheet for each of the following results. Your scores will go in the "WE" and your opponents' scores will go in the "THEY" column.

i) North deals (neither side is vulnerable). East-West bid to a contract of Three No Trump and take the required nine tricks.

ii) East deals (East-West are vulnerable). North-South bid to a contract of Four Spades and take exactly ten tricks.

iii) South deals (North-South are vulnerable). East-West bid to a contract of One Diamond and take nine tricks (two overtricks).

iv) West deals (both sides are vulnerable). North-South bid to a contract of Four Hearts and take eleven tricks (one overtrick).

WE | THEY

Which side won the round? By how much?

_____   _____

EXERCISE THREE: FOR THE CURIOUS (RUBBER BRIDGE SCORING)

Using the same four results as in the previous exercise, record them on a score sheet using Rubber Bridge scoring.

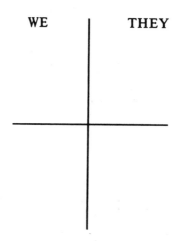

WE | THEY

Which side won the rubber? By how much?

_____   _____

JOY OF BRIDGE SCORING

TRICK SCORE

____ points per trick bid and made in Diamonds or Clubs

____ points per trick bid and made in Spades or Hearts

____ points for the first trick bid and made in No Trump

____ points for each additional trick bid and made in No Trump

BONUSES

____ points for bidding and making a not-vulnerable Game

____ points for bidding and making a vulnerable Game

____ points for bidding and making a Part-Game

PENALTIES

____ points per trick not vulnerable

____ points per trick vulnerable

GAME CONTRACTS

Game in No Trump: _____

Game in a Major Suit: _____

Game in a Minor Suit: _____

UNIT FOUR: THE CAPTAIN

Joy of Bridge reference: pages 34 - 46

Once a partner opens the bidding, the partnership, in the language of bidding, exchanges enough information to come to a consensus which solves two problems:

- **HOW HIGH** should the contract be (Part-Game, Game or Slam)?

- **WHERE** should the contract be played (Clubs, Diamonds, Hearts, Spades, No Trump)?

EXERCISE ONE: RELATING POINTS AND TRICKS

How many combined points would the partnership need to take all the tricks?

_____

How many combined points would the partnership need to make a contract of Three No Trump? Four Hearts? Four Spades? Five Clubs? Five Diamonds?

_____   _____   _____   _____   _____

EXERCISE TWO: HOW HIGH

Review the requirements for an opening bid of One No Trump.

Suppose your partner opens the bidding One No Trump. With each of the following hands, do you have enough points to go for a Game bonus? Answer yes, no or maybe.

1) ♠ A Q 3
    ♡ Q J 2
    ◇ J 8 4 3
    ♣ Q 10 8

    _____

2) ♠ J 9 3
    ♡ Q 7 2
    ◇ A 6 4
    ♣ Q 5 3 2

    _____

3) ♠ 8 6
    ♡ J 10 3
    ◇ K J 9 8
    ♣ 9 8 5 3

    _____

EXERCISE THREE: THE MAGIC FIT

What is the minimum number of cards in a suit that the partnership must hold to ensure that they have the majority?

_____

How many cards in a suit are required for the partnership to want to play with that suit as trump?

_____

EXERCISE FOUR: WHERE

Suppose your partner opens the bidding One No Trump. Do you have a Magic Major Suit Fit with any of the following hands? Answer yes, no or maybe.

1) ♠ Q 3
    ♡ A 8
    ♢ A Q 9 7 4
    ♣ J 9 7 3

2) ♠ Q 8 6 5 4 2
    ♡ 7 2
    ♢ Q 6 3
    ♣ 9 3

3) ♠ 9 8
    ♡ K Q 10 3 2
    ♢ A 7 3
    ♣ 5 3 2

_____   _____   _____

If your partner opens the bidding One No Trump, how many cards must you have in a suit to be certain that you have a Magic Fit? How few cards must you have in a suit to be certain that you do not have a Magic Fit?

_____   _____

LET'S EXPERIMENT

Construct the following hand, and place it face-up on the table:

Hand #1

```
                    ♠ A J 7
                    ♡ A 7 6
                    ♢ K 5
                    ♣ A 10 9 6 5

   ♠ 10 9 8 5            N              ♠ 6 4 3
   ♡ 8 5                                ♡ K Q J 10 9
   ♢ Q J 10 9 4    W         E          ♢ A 6 3 2
   ♣ 4 2                S               ♣ 3

                    ♠ K Q 2
                    ♡ 4 3 2
                    ♢ 8 7
                    ♣ K Q J 8 7
```

Assume that North is the dealer. What would be North's opening bid?

_____

Assuming that East says Pass, what would South's response be?

_____

Assuming that West, North and East all say Pass, what is the final contract?

_____

Who will be declarer? Who will be dummy? Who will make the opening lead?

_____   _____   _____

Which card should be led by the opening leader?

_____

How many tricks does declarer need to make his contract?

_____

Have each player pick up his hand. Start the bidding with North and complete the auction. Then play out the hand.

Did declarer take enough tricks to make the contract? How should declarer plan to play in a No Trump contract when he has enough sure tricks to fulfill the contract?

_____

Now construct the following hand, and place it face-up on the table:

Hand #2

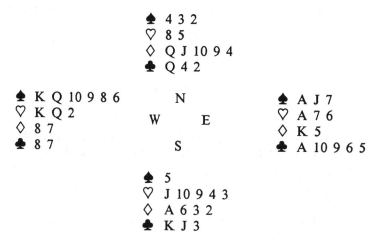

♠ 4 3 2
♡ 8 5
◇ Q J 10 9 4
♣ Q 4 2

♠ K Q 10 9 8 6   N   ♠ A J 7
♡ K Q 2   ♡ A 7 6
◇ 8 7   W   E   ◇ K 5
♣ 8 7   ♣ A 10 9 6 5
                        S

♠ 5
♡ J 10 9 4 3
◇ A 6 3 2
♣ K J 3

Assume that East is the dealer. What would be East's opening bid?

_____

Assuming that South says Pass, what would West's response be?

_____

Assuming that North, East and South all say Pass, what is the final contract?

_____

Who will be declarer? Who will be dummy? Who will make the opening lead?

_____   _____   _____

Which card should be led by the opening leader?

_____

How many tricks does declarer need to make his contract?

_____

Have each player pick up his hand. Start the bidding with East and complete the auction. Then play out the hand.

Did declarer take enough tricks to make the contract? How should declarer plan to play in a Trump contract when he has enough sure tricks to fulfill the contract?

_____

SUMMARY

HOW HIGH

THE KEY QUESTION FOR DECIDING HOW HIGH

Do we have _____ combined points?

If the answer is YES: Play in a _____ contract.

If the answer is NO: Play in a _____ contract.

WHERE

THE KEY QUESTION FOR DECIDING WHERE WHEN BIDDING TO A GAME CONTRACT

Do we have a _____?

If the answer is YES: Play in _____ or _____.

If the answer is NO: Play in _____.

THE KEY QUESTION FOR DECIDING WHERE WHEN BIDDING TO A PART-GAME CONTRACT

Do we have any _____?

If the answer is YES: Play Part-Game in _____.

If the answer is NO: Play Part-Game in _____.

UNIT FIVE: RESPONDING TO A ONE NO TRUMP OPENING

Joy of Bridge reference: pages 47 - 58

The One No Trump opening is a highly limited bid since it shows a narrow point range and balanced distribution. It should be easy for responder to add up the combined hands to determine HOW HIGH and WHERE to play the hand.

Responder asks: "Are there 26 combined points?" and "Do we have a Magic Fit?"

EXERCISE ONE: RESPONDING WITH 0 - 7 POINTS

Suppose your partner opens the bidding One No Trump. Consider each of the following hands which you might hold as responder. HOW HIGH should the contract be played in each case (Part-Game or Game)? WHERE should the contract be played in each case? What should responder bid with each hand?

1) ♠ Q 7
    ♡ 9 3 2
    ◊ Q 6 4 2
    ♣ J 8 7 6

2) ♠ 9 8 7 5 4 3
    ♡ 7
    ◊ J 7 5 3
    ♣ 8 6

3) ♠ 9 3
    ♡ 8 2
    ◊ K 10 7 6 3
    ♣ Q 9 5 2

	1)	2)	3)
HCP:	_____	_____	_____
+ Length Points:	_____	_____	_____
= Total Points:	_____	_____	_____
How High:	_____	_____	_____
Where:	_____	_____	_____
Bid:	_____	_____	_____

How are these hands similar? How are they different?

EXERCISE TWO: RESPONDING WITH 8 - 9 POINTS

Suppose your partner opens the bidding One No Trump. HOW HIGH do you want to play the following hands (Part-Game, Game or Maybe Game)? WHERE do you want to play the hands? What response can you make that will tell opener HOW HIGH and WHERE you would like to play the hand?

1) ♠ K J 3
   ♡ Q 2
   ◇ Q 7 6 3
   ♣ J 8 3 2

   HCP: _____
   + Length Points: _____
   = Total Points: _____

   How High: _____
   Where: _____
   Bid: _____

2) ♠ A 8
   ♡ 7 6 4
   ◇ Q J 10 9 8
   ♣ 10 8 4

   HCP: _____
   + Length Points: _____
   = Total Points: _____

   How High: _____
   Where: _____
   Bid: _____

3) ♠ 4 3 2
   ♡ 6 5
   ◇ 8 7
   ♣ A K 9 7 5 2

   HCP: _____
   + Length Points: _____
   = Total Points: _____

   How High: _____
   Where: _____
   Bid: _____

EXERCISE THREE: RESPONDING WITH 10 - 14 POINTS

Suppose your partner opens the bidding One No Trump. HOW HIGH do you want to play each of the following hands (Part-Game, Game or Maybe Game)? Do you have a Magic Major Suit Fit (yes, no or maybe)? What response should you make on each hand?

1) ♠ K 7
   ♡ Q 5
   ◇ K Q 4 2
   ♣ J 9 6 4 3

   HCP: _____
   + Length Points: _____
   = Total Points: _____

   How High: _____
   Magic Fit: _____
   Bid: _____

2) ♠ A 3
   ♡ Q J 8 6 4 3
   ◇ 7 4
   ♣ J 6 2

   HCP: _____
   + Length Points: _____
   = Total Points: _____

   How High: _____
   Magic Fit: _____
   Bid: _____

3) ♠ 5 4
   ♡ 7 6
   ◇ J 8 7
   ♣ A K 8 7 5 3

   HCP: _____
   + Length Points: _____
   = Total Points: _____

   How High: _____
   Magic Fit: _____
   Bid: _____

EXERCISE FOUR: RESPONDING WHEN YOU KNOW HOW HIGH BUT NOT WHERE

Suppose your partner opens the bidding One No Trump. HOW HIGH do you want to play each of the following hands (Part-Game, Game or Maybe Game)? Do you have a Magic Major Suit Fit (yes, no or maybe)? What information do you need from your partner to determine WHERE to play the hand? What response should you make to ask partner for this information?

1) ♠ K 9 7 5 3
   ♡ A 2
   ◇ J 6 3
   ♣ Q 5 2

   HCP: _____
   + Length Points: _____
   = Total Points: _____

   How High: _____
   Magic Fit: _____
   Bid: _____

2) ♠ A 8
   ♡ Q J 9 5 2
   ◇ 8 3
   ♣ A 6 4 2

   HCP: _____
   + Length Points: _____
   = Total Points: _____

   How High: _____
   Magic Fit: _____
   Bid: _____

LET'S EXPERIMENT

Construct the following hand, and place it face-up on the table:

Hand #3

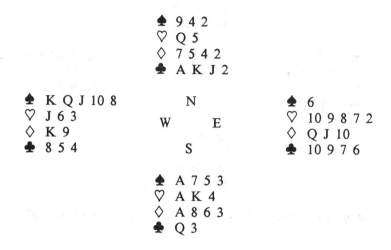

```
                        ♠ 9 4 2
                        ♡ Q 5
                        ◇ 7 5 4 2
                        ♣ A K J 2

    ♠ K Q J 10 8              N              ♠ 6
    ♡ J 6 3                                  ♡ 10 9 8 7 2
    ◇ K 9            W              E        ◇ Q J 10
    ♣ 8 5 4                                  ♣ 10 9 7 6
                             S
                        ♠ A 7 5 3
                        ♡ A K 4
                        ◇ A 8 6 3
                        ♣ Q 3
```

Assume that South is the dealer. What would be South's opening bid?

_____

Assuming that West says Pass, what would North's response be?

_____

Assuming that East says Pass, what will South do next? What will be the final contract?

_____   _____

Who will be declarer? Who will be dummy? Who will make the opening lead?

_____   _____   _____

Which card should be led by the opening leader?

_____

How many tricks does declarer need to make his contract?

_____

Have each player pick up his hand. Start the bidding with South and complete the auction. Then play out the hand.

Did declarer take enough tricks to make the contract? What guideline is useful when declarer is taking his sure tricks?

_____

Now construct the following hand, and place it face-up on the table:

Hand #4

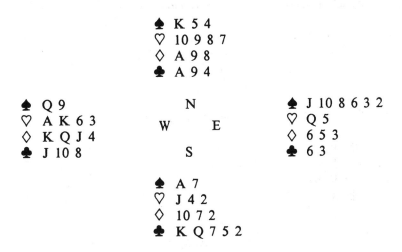

```
                          ♠ K 5 4
                          ♡ 10 9 8 7
                          ◇ A 9 8
                          ♣ A 9 4

      ♠ Q 9                   N              ♠ J 10 8 6 3 2
      ♡ A K 6 3                              ♡ Q 5
      ◇ K Q J 4           W       E          ◇ 6 5 3
      ♣ J 10 8                               ♣ 6 3
                          S
                          ♠ A 7
                          ♡ J 4 2
                          ◇ 10 7 2
                          ♣ K Q 7 5 2
```

Assume that West is the dealer. What would be West's opening bid?

———————

Assuming that North says Pass, what would East bid?

———————

Assuming that South says Pass, what does West do next? Why? What will the final contract be?

———————   ————————————————   ———————

Who will be declarer? Who will be dummy? Who will make the opening lead?

———————   ———————   ———————

Which card should be led by the opening leader?

———————

How many tricks does declarer need to make his contract?

———————

Have each player pick up his hand. Start the bidding with West and complete the auction. Then play out the hand.

Did declarer take enough tricks to make the contract? What method can declarer use to establish the additional tricks needed to make the contract?

——————————————————————————————

RESPONSES TO AN OPENING BID OF ONE NO TRUMP

With 0 - 7 points: Bid _____ or _____ or

_____ with a 5-card suit or longer.

Otherwise, _____.

With 8 - 9 points: Bid _____.

With 10 - 14 points: Bid _____ or _____ with a

6-card or longer Major suit.

Bid _____ or _____ with a

5-card Major suit.

Otherwise, bid _____.

UNIT SIX: THE MESSAGES OF BIDDING

Joy of Bridge reference: pages 59 - 63

Every bid carries a message telling partner either to bid or not to bid or to make the decision himself. A sign-off bid tells partner not to bid again. A forcing bid tells partner he must bid again. An invitational bid says he must make a choice. A marathon bid says he must continue to bid until a Game contract is reached.

EXERCISE ONE: THE SIGN-OFF BID (THE STOP SIGN)

After a One No Trump opening bid, which four of the following responses are sign-off bids?

Two Hearts	Three No Trump	Two No Trump
Four Spades	Three Hearts	Two Diamonds

_____   _____   _____   _____

EXERCISE TWO: THE INVITATIONAL BID (THE YIELD SIGN)

After a One No Trump opening bid, which response is invitational? Why?

_____   _____

EXERCISE THREE: THE FORCING BID (THE GO SIGN)

What are two forcing bids in response to a One No Trump opening bid?

_____   _____

EXERCISE FOUR: FORCING TO GAME (THE MARATHON BID)

What marathon bids do you already know?

_____   _____

LET'S EXPERIMENT

Construct the following hand, and place it face-up on the table:

Hand #5

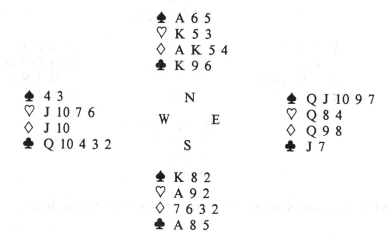

```
                        ♠ A 6 5
                        ♡ K 5 3
                        ◇ A K 5 4
                        ♣ K 9 6
        ♠ 4 3                N            ♠ Q J 10 9 7
        ♡ J 10 7 6                        ♡ Q 8 4
        ◇ J 10           W       E        ◇ Q 9 8
        ♣ Q 10 4 3 2         S            ♣ J 7
                        ♠ K 8 2
                        ♡ A 9 2
                        ◇ 7 6 3 2
                        ♣ A 8 5
```

Assume that North is the dealer. What would be North's opening bid?

_____

Assuming that East says Pass, what would South's response be? Is South's response a sign-off, an invitational bid or a forcing bid?

_____   _____

Assuming that West says Pass, what will North do next? What will be the final contract?

_____   _____

Who will be declarer? Who will be dummy? Who will make the opening lead?

_____   _____   _____

Which card should be led by the opening leader?

_____

How many tricks does declarer need to make his contract?

_____

Have each player pick up his hand. Start the bidding with North and complete the auction. Then play out the hand.

Did declarer take enough tricks to make the contract? What method can declarer use to establish the additional trick needed to make the contract?

_____

Now construct the following hand, and place it face-up on the table:

Hand #6

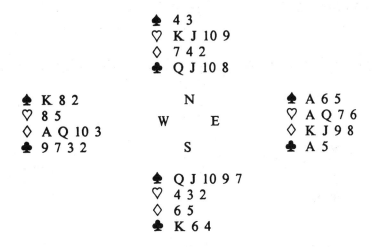

Assume that East is the dealer. What would be the opening bid?

_____

Assuming that South says Pass, what would West bid? Is this a sign-off bid, an invitational bid or a forcing bid?

_____   _____

Assuming that North says Pass, what does East do next? Why? What will be the final contract?

_____   _____   _____

Who will be declarer? Who will be dummy? Who will make the opening lead?

_____   _____   _____

Which card should be led by the opening leader?

_____

How many tricks does declarer need to make his contract?

_____

Have each player pick up his hand. Start the bidding with East and complete the auction. Then play out the hand.

Did declarer take enough tricks to make the contract? What method can declarer use to establish the additional trick needed to make the contract?

_____

BIDDING MESSAGES

Sign-off: Partner must _____.

Invitational: Partner may _____ or _____.

Forcing: Partner must _____.

Marathon: The partnership keeps bidding until _____.

UNIT SEVEN: RESPONDING TO OPENING BIDS OF ONE IN A SUIT

Joy of Bridge reference: pages 64 - 79

One-level opening bids in a suit . . . One Club, One Diamond, One Heart and One Spade . . . are very common. They are much less specific than One No Trump, both in point range and possible hand distributions.

Responder cannot answer HOW HIGH and WHERE right away without more information about opener's hand. So responder makes a bid that tells opener something about his hand, giving opener an opportunity to further describe his hand. Responder uses four questions to help him determine the appropriate response.

EXERCISE ONE: FIRST QUESTION - CAN I RAISE PARTNER'S MAJOR?

Review the requirements for an opening bid of one in a suit.
Construct a hand which would open the bidding One Heart.

If opener bids One Heart, how many Hearts must responder hold to be certain that there is a Magic Major Suit Fit?

_____

If opener bids One Heart, how many points must responder hold to be certain that there is enough combined strength for Game?

_____

As responder, what would you think about the following hand if partner opened the bidding One Heart? What if partner opened One Spade?

$$\spadesuit \ 10 \ 7 \ 6 \ 4$$
$$\heartsuit \ -$$
$$\diamondsuit \ 9 \ 8 \ 7 \ 4$$
$$\clubsuit \ A \ 9 \ 6 \ 4 \ 3$$

_____

What are the values of your short suits when counting dummy points? When do you use dummy points?

Void: ____ points   Singleton: ____ points   Doubleton: ____ points

_____

Your partner opens the bidding One Spade. Determine your response on each of the following hands:

1) ♠ Q 9 7 6
    ♡ A 7 6 3
    ◇ -
    ♣ A 10 6 5 3

    Dummy Points: _____
    Response: _____

2) ♠ K 10 7 3
    ♡ 9 7 4
    ◇ 5 4
    ♣ K Q 7 6

    Dummy Points: _____
    Response: _____

3) ♠ A J 9 3
    ♡ 9
    ◇ Q 9 7 4
    ♣ Q 10 5 3

    Dummy Points: _____
    Response: _____

EXERCISE TWO: SECOND QUESTION - DO I HAVE A WEAK HAND (0 - 5 POINTS)?

What would you respond with the following hand if opener bid One Club?

            ♠ 8 7 5 2
            ♡ J 2
            ◇ Q 9 5 3
            ♣ 10 6 3

            Response: _____

EXERCISE THREE: THIRD QUESTION - CAN I BID A NEW SUIT AT THE ONE-LEVEL?

Your partner opens the bidding One Club. What should you respond with each of the following hands?

1) ♠ 9 6 4 2
    ♡ K 8 4
    ◇ Q 4
    ♣ Q J 6 3

    Response: _____

2) ♠ Q 8 7 4 2
    ♡ K J 7 5 3
    ◇ 9
    ♣ K 5

    Response: _____

3) ♠ A K 6 3
    ♡ Q 5 3 2
    ◇ Q 6 3
    ♣ J 7

    Response: _____

EXERCISE FOUR: FOURTH QUESTION - DO I HAVE A MINIMUM HAND (6 - 10 POINTS)?

Your partner opens the bidding One Spade. What should you respond with each of the following hands?

1) ♠ J 8
    ♡ K 9
    ◇ K 9 7 3
    ♣ J 8 5 3 2

    Response: _____

2) ♠ 9 6 3
    ♡ K 10 4
    ◇ 8 5 2
    ♣ Q J 7 5

    Response: _____

3) ♠ 7
    ♡ 9 3
    ◇ 8 7 2
    ♣ K J 8 6 5 4 2

    Response: _____

EXERCISE FIVE: THE FINAL CHOICE

Your partner opens the bidding One Spade. What should you respond with each of the following hands?

1) ♠ A 3
    ♡ 8 5 3
    ◇ Q J 9 6 3
    ♣ K J 3

    Response: _____

2) ♠ K 7
    ♡ K 10 8 7 6
    ◇ A J 8 6 2
    ♣ J

    Response: _____

3) ♠ 9 7
    ♡ K 6 3
    ◇ A 5 3 2
    ♣ K Q 6 4

    Response: _____

EXERCISE SIX: RAISING OPENER'S MINOR

Your partner opens the bidding One Diamond. What should you respond with each of the following hands?

1) ♠ K 5 4
    ♡ 8 5
    ◇ J 9 6 4 3
    ♣ Q 8 2

    Response: _____

2) ♠ A 3
    ♡ 8 5 3
    ◇ Q J 9 6 3
    ♣ K J 3

    Response: _____

3) ♠ K 7
    ♡ K 10
    ◇ A J 8 6 3 2
    ♣ J 6 3

    Response: _____

EXERCISE SEVEN: PUTTING IT ALL TOGETHER

Your partner opens the bidding One Heart. Use Responder's Four Questions to determine the appropriate response on each of the following hands:

1) ♠ A 7 6 4 3
    ♡ K 7 5 2
    ◇ 9 8
    ♣ K 6

    Response: _____

2) ♠ J 8 3
    ♡ 9 6
    ◇ Q 8 6 5 3 2
    ♣ 6 2

    Response: _____

3) ♠ J 7 5 2
    ♡ 8 4
    ◇ 7 2
    ♣ A Q J 6 3

    Response: _____

4) ♠ Q 7
    ♡ 7 3
    ◇ K 9 5 4 3
    ♣ J 6 4 2

    Response: _____

5) ♠ A 8
    ♡ Q 9 4
    ◇ A J 7 4
    ♣ Q 9 6 3

    Response: _____

6) ♠ 8 7 6
    ♡ A K Q J
    ◇ 9 4 3
    ♣ 10 7 3

    Response: _____

LET'S EXPERIMENT

Construct the following hand, and place it face-up on the table:

Hand #7

                          ♠ Q 4 3
                          ♡ 9 8 7 6
                          ◇ A 3
                          ♣ A K J 4

   ♠ J 10 9   N   ♠ A K 7 6
   ♡ -   ♡ 5 4 3 2
   ◇ K 10 8 7 4   W   E   ◇ Q J 9
   ♣ 10 8 6 5 3   ♣ 9 7
                             S

                          ♠ 8 5 2
                          ♡ A K Q J 10
                          ◇ 6 5 2
                          ♣ Q 2

Assume that South is the dealer. What would be South's opening bid?

Assuming that West says Pass, what would North's response be?

—————————

Assuming that East, South and West say Pass, what will be the final contract?

—————————

Which card should be led by the opening leader?

—————————

How many tricks does declarer need to make his contract?

—————————

Have each player pick up his hand. Start the bidding with South and complete the auction. Then play out the hand.

Did declarer take enough tricks to make the contract? Which suit should declarer play first when he has enough sure tricks to make his contract? When taking his sure tricks in the Club suit, what must declarer be careful to do?

—————————   ————————————   ————————————

Now construct the following hand, and place it face-up on the table:

Hand #8

```
                          ♠ 5 3
                          ♡ Q J 10 9
                          ◇ 9 7 6 5
                          ♣ A Q 2

     ♠ A Q J 10 9              N              ♠ K 8 7 6
     ♡ 6 5 2                                  ♡ K 8 7
     ◇ A K 2          W              E        ◇ 4 3
     ♣ 7 3                                    ♣ 9 8 6 5
                              S
                          ♠ 4 2
                          ♡ A 4 3
                          ◇ Q J 10 8
                          ♣ K J 10 4
```

Assume that West is the dealer. What bid will he make?

—————————

Assuming that North says Pass, what would East bid?

—————————

Assuming that South, West and North all say Pass, what is the final contract?

—————————

What should the opening lead be?

_____

How many tricks does declarer need to make his contract?

_____

Have each player pick up his hand. Start the bidding with West and complete the auction. Then play out the hand.

Did declarer take enough tricks to make the contract? What method can declarer use to establish additional tricks when playing in a trump contract that is not available in a No Trump contract?

_____   _____

SUMMARY

RESPONDER'S FOUR QUESTIONS

1. **CAN I RAISE PARTNER'S MAJOR?**

    If the answer is YES: Revalue your hand using _____
    points and raise to the appropriate level.

    0 - 5 points: _____.

    6 - 10 points: Raise to the _____.

    11 - 12 points: Raise to the _____.

    13 - 16 points: Raise to the _____.

2. **DO I HAVE A WEAK HAND (0 - 5 POINTS)?**

    If the answer is YES: _____.

3. **CAN I BID A NEW SUIT AT THE ONE-LEVEL?**

    If the answer is YES: Bid _____.

4. **DO I HAVE A MINIMUM HAND (6 - 10 POINTS)?**

    If the answer is YES: Raise opener's Minor suit to the _____
    with 4-card support.

    Bid _____.

    If the answer is NO: Raise opener's Minor suit to the _____
    with 11 - 12 points and 4-card support.

    Raise opener's Minor suit to _____
    with 13 - 16 points and 4-card support.

    Bid _____.

UNIT EIGHT: OPENER'S REBID AFTER A ONE-LEVEL RESPONSE

Joy of Bridge reference: pages 80 - 94

Opener acts as the describer. He describes his hand to the responder who, as captain, uses the information to decide HOW HIGH and WHERE to place the contract. Opener's original bid started the description. After hearing responder's bid, opener can make a second bid which tells responder more about the strength and shape of opener's hand. Opener's second bid is called opener's rebid.

To help opener determine his best rebid, he classifies the strength of his hand into:

> Minimum hand: 13 - 16 points
> Medium hand: 17 - 18 points
> Maximum hand: 19 - 21 points

Opener then uses four questions to help him determine the appropriate rebid.

EXERCISE ONE: OPENER CLASSIFIES HIS STRENGTH

Work as a group to create three hands which would be opened One Heart. Make the first one a minimum hand. Write it down.

Change a few cards to make it a medium hand. Write it down.

Change a few more cards to make it a maximum hand. Write it down.

Minimum	Medium	Maximum
Spades	Spades	Spades
Hearts	Hearts	Hearts
Diamonds	Diamonds	Diamonds
Clubs	Clubs	Clubs

EXERCISE TWO: FIRST QUESTION - CAN I RAISE PARTNER'S MAJOR?

You open the bidding One Diamond and your partner responds One Spade. How would you classify the strength of each hand (minimum, medium or maximum)? What would you rebid with each of the following hands?

1) ♠ J 8 6 4
   ♡ A 9
   ◇ A K J 6 3
   ♣ 5 3

   Strength: _____
   Rebid: _____

2) ♠ A Q 8 4
   ♡ 9
   ◇ A K 8 7
   ♣ K Q 7 4

   Strength: _____
   Rebid: _____

3) ♠ K J 7 3
   ♡ K 8 7
   ◇ A Q J 8 3
   ♣ 10

   Strength: _____
   Rebid: _____

EXERCISE THREE: SECOND QUESTION - CAN I BID A NEW SUIT AT THE ONE-LEVEL?

You open the bidding One Club and your partner responds One Diamond. How would you classify the strength of each hand (minimum, medium or maximum)? What would you rebid with each of the following hands?

1) ♠ K J 7 2
   ♡ K 8 4
   ◇ 8 3
   ♣ A Q 6 3

   Strength: _____
   Rebid: _____

2) ♠ A J 8 3
   ♡ K Q 6 4
   ◇ -
   ♣ K Q J 7 3

   Strength: _____
   Rebid: _____

3) ♠ A K J 9
   ♡ 4 3
   ◇ A 7
   ♣ A K 7 4 3

   Strength: _____
   Rebid: _____

EXERCISE FOUR: THIRD QUESTION - IS MY HAND BALANCED?

You open the bidding One Diamond and your partner responds One Heart. How would you classify the strength of each hand (minimum, medium or maximum)? What would you rebid with each of the following hands?

1) ♠ A J 10
   ♡ Q 7
   ◇ K J 9 7 3
   ♣ Q 7 4

   Strength: _____
   Rebid: _____

2) ♠ K Q 7
   ♡ A J 9
   ◇ A Q J 9
   ♣ K 10 4

   Strength: _____
   Rebid: _____

3) ♠ K 8 6 2
   ♡ K 8
   ◇ A J 9 6
   ♣ Q J 9

   Strength: _____
   Rebid: _____

EXERCISE FIVE: FOURTH QUESTION - SHOULD I BID A NEW SUIT AT THE TWO-LEVEL?

You open the bidding One Diamond and your partner responds One Spade. How would you classify the strength of each hand (minimum, medium or maximum)? What would you rebid with each of the following hands?

1) ♠ 2
   ♡ Q 3
   ◇ A Q 9 8 4
   ♣ K J 7 3 2

   Strength: _____
   Rebid: _____

2) ♠ J 8
   ♡ K 7
   ◇ K Q J 7 5
   ♣ A Q 9 2

   Strength: _____
   Rebid: _____

3) ♠ K 9
   ♡ 4
   ◇ A K J 9 7 2
   ♣ A K 9 4

   Strength: _____
   Rebid: _____

4) ♠ 10 3
    ♡ K 9
    ◇ A Q J 9 3 2
    ♣ Q J 3

5) ♠ J
    ♡ K 8 4
    ◇ A K J 8 4 3 2
    ♣ K 8

6) ♠ J 8
    ♡ A 9 4 2
    ◇ K J 8 7 3
    ♣ A 3

Strength: _____
Rebid: _____

Strength: _____
Rebid: _____

Strength: _____
Rebid: _____

LET'S EXPERIMENT

Construct the following hand, and place it face-up on the table:

Hand #9

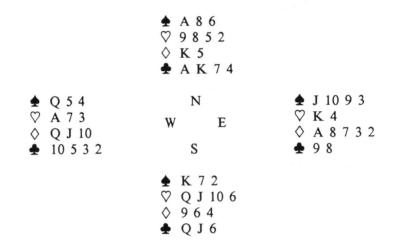

Assume that North is the dealer. What would be North's opening bid?

_____

Assuming that East says Pass, what would South's response be?

_____

Assuming that West says Pass, what would North's rebid be?

_____

Assuming that East, South and West all say Pass, what is the final contract?

_____

Which card should be led by the opening leader? How many tricks does declarer need to make his contract?

_____   _____

Have each player pick up his hand. Start the bidding with North and complete the auction. Then play out the hand.

Did declarer take enough tricks to make the contract? What should declarer do before trying to take his sure tricks?

_____   _____

What problem will declarer sometimes encounter when trying to draw trumps?

_____

Now construct the following hand, and place it face-up on the table:

Hand #10

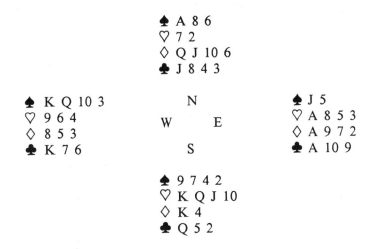

```
                    ♠ A 8 6
                    ♡ 7 2
                    ◇ Q J 10 6
                    ♣ J 8 4 3

    ♠ K Q 10 3          N           ♠ J 5
    ♡ 9 6 4                         ♡ A 8 5 3
    ◇ 8 5 3         W       E       ◇ A 9 7 2
    ♣ K 7 6             S           ♣ A 10 9

                    ♠ 9 7 4 2
                    ♡ K Q J 10
                    ◇ K 4
                    ♣ Q 5 2
```

Assume that East is the dealer. What would be East's opening bid?

_____

Assuming that South says Pass, what would West's response be?

_____

Assuming that North says Pass, what would East's rebid be?

_____

Assuming that South, West and North all say Pass, what is the final contract?

_____

Which card should be led by the opening leader?

_____

What information does the card lead by South give to his partner, North?

_____

How many tricks does declarer need to make his contract?

_____

Have each player pick up his hand. Start the bidding with East and complete the auction. Then play out the hand.

Did declarer take enough tricks to make the contract? How can declarer establish the additional tricks needed to make his contract?

_____   _____

OPENER'S FOUR QUESTIONS

1. CAN I RAISE PARTNER'S MAJOR?

    If the answer is YES: Revalue your hand using dummy points and
    raise to the appropriate level.

    13 - 16 points: Raise to the _____.

    17 - 18 points: Raise to the _____.

    19 - 21 points: Raise to the _____.

2. CAN I BID A NEW SUIT AT THE ONE-LEVEL?

    If the answer is YES: Bid the new suit at the appropriate level.

    13 - 18 points: Bid at the _____.

    19 - 21 points: Bid at the _____.

3. IS MY HAND BALANCED?

    If the answer is YES: Rebid No Trump at the appropriate level.

    13 - 15 points: Stay at the _____.

    19 - 21 points: Jump to the _____.

4. SHOULD I BID A NEW SUIT AT THE TWO LEVEL?

    If the answer is YES: Bid the new suit at the appropriate level.

    13 - 16 points: Bid at the _____. *

    17 - 18 points: Bid at the _____.

    19 - 21 points: Bid at the _____.

    If the answer is NO: Rebid your first suit at the appropriate level
    or raise partner's Minor.

    13 - 16 points: Bid at the _____.

    17 - 18 points: Bid at the _____.

    19 - 21 points: Bid at the _____ (Major)

    or _____ (Minor).

* Only bid a new suit if it is lower-ranking than your first suit.

UNIT NINE: OPENER'S REBID AFTER A TWO-LEVEL RESPONSE

Joy of Bridge reference: pages 95 - 104

Opener's rebid after the response of a new suit at the two-level is similar to the rebid after a new suit at the one-level. Opener is the describer.

Responder's bid of a new suit at the two-level is forcing. Opener must bid again to tell responder enough about his strength and distribution that responder will be in a position to decide HOW HIGH and WHERE to place the contract. Opener continues to use Opener's Four Questions to guide him to the appropriate rebid.

EXERCISE ONE: OPENER'S REBID AFTER A TWO-LEVEL RESPONSE

You open the bidding One Heart and your partner responds Two Clubs. Use Opener's Four Questions to decide what to rebid on each of the following hands:

1) ♠ K 7 2
    ♡ A Q J 9 3 2
    ◇ J 8
    ♣ 7 4

    Rebid: _____

2) ♠ 10 7
    ♡ K Q 8 7 3
    ◇ A Q J 8
    ♣ Q 8

    Rebid: _____

3) ♠ 9 6
    ♡ A K J 10 8 7 3
    ◇ A K
    ♣ J 7

    Rebid: _____

EXERCISE TWO: MORE REBIDS AFTER A TWO-LEVEL RESPONSE

You open the bidding One Spade and your partner responds Two Hearts. Use Opener's Four Questions to decide what to rebid on each of the following hands:

1) ♠ A Q 8 7 3
    ♡ K J 8 6
    ◇ K 8
    ♣ 7 2

    Rebid: _____

2) ♠ A Q J 7 2
    ♡ 8 6
    ◇ K J 6
    ♣ Q 10 2

    Rebid: _____

3) ♠ A Q 9 8 4
    ♡ 9 3
    ◇ K 4
    ♣ K J 7 3

    Rebid: _____

4) ♠ K Q J 9 2
    ♡ A J 10 3
    ◇ K 8 7
    ♣ 4

    Rebid: _____

5) ♠ Q 10 8 6 3
    ♡ K 9
    ◇ A Q 10
    ♣ A K J

    Rebid: _____

6) ♠ A K 10 9 6
    ♡ J 9
    ◇ A K 9 8 7
    ♣ 3

    Rebid: _____

Construct the following hand, and place it face-up on the table:

Hand #11

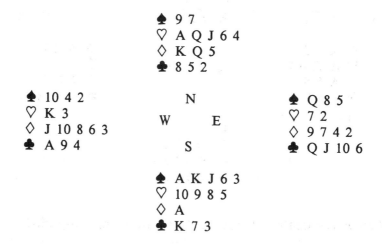

Assume that South is the dealer. What would be South's opening bid?

_____

Assuming that West says Pass, what would North's response be?

_____

Assuming that East says Pass, what would South's rebid be? (Don't forget to use dummy points.)

_____

Assuming that West, North and East all say Pass, what is the final contract?

_____

Which card should be led by the opening leader?

_____

Have each player pick up his hand. Start the bidding with South and complete the auction. Then play out the hand.

Did declarer take enough tricks to make the contract? How can declarer avoid losing a trump trick?

_____   _____

Would it make a difference if West had started with the K 7 3 of Hearts? Which card should declarer lead from dummy to allow for this possibility?

_____   _____

Now construct the following hand, and place it face-up on the table:

Hand #12

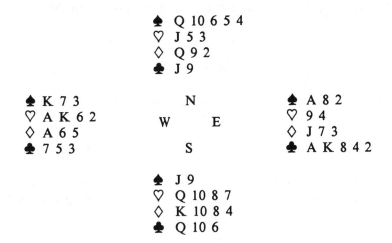

```
                        ♠ Q 10 6 5 4
                        ♡ J 5 3
                        ◇ Q 9 2
                        ♣ J 9

        ♠ K 7 3              N              ♠ A 8 2
        ♡ A K 6 2                           ♡ 9 4
        ◇ A 6 5         W         E         ◇ J 7 3
        ♣ 7 5 3              S              ♣ A K 8 4 2

                        ♠ J 9
                        ♡ Q 10 8 7
                        ◇ K 10 8 4
                        ♣ Q 10 6
```

Assume that West is the dealer. What would be West's opening bid?

_____

Assuming that North says Pass, what would East's response be?

_____

Assuming that South says Pass, what would West's rebid be?

_____

Assume that North says Pass and East raises West's rebid to Game. South, East and North all say Pass. What is the final contract? Who is declarer?

_____   _____

Which card should be led by the opening leader? Why?

_____   _____

Have each player pick up his hand. Start the bidding with West and complete the auction. Then play out the hand.

Did declarer take enough tricks to make the contract? How can declarer establish the additional tricks needed to make his contract?

_____   _____

Should declarer win the first trick in dummy (with the Ace of Spades) or in his hand (with the King of Spades)? Why?

_____   _____

OPENER'S FOUR QUESTIONS

1. CAN I RAISE PARTNER'S MAJOR?

   If the answer is YES: Revalue your hand using dummy points and raise to the appropriate level.

          13 - 16 points: Raise to the _____.

          17 - 18 points: Raise to the _____.

          19 - 21 points: Raise to the _____.

2. CAN I BID A NEW SUIT AT THE ONE-LEVEL?

   The answer is always NO after a response at the two-level.

3. IS MY HAND BALANCED?

   If the answer is YES: Rebid No Trump at the appropriate level.

          13 - 15 points: Stay at the _____.

          19 - 21 points: Jump to the _____.

4. SHOULD I BID A NEW SUIT AT THE TWO LEVEL?

   If the answer is YES: Bid the new suit at the appropriate level.

          13 - 16 points: Bid your second suit. *

          17 - 18 points: Bid your second suit.

          19 - 21 points: _____ in your second suit.

   If the answer is NO: Rebid your first suit at the appropriate level or raise partner's Minor.

          13 - 16 points: Bid at the _____

                       or raise to the _____.

          17 - 18 points: Bid at the _____

                       or raise to the _____.

          19 - 21 points: Bid _____ in your suit

                       or raise to the _____.

* Only bid a new suit if it is lower-ranking than your first suit and you can bid it at the two-level.

UNIT TEN: OPENER'S REBID AFTER A RAISE

Joy of Bridge reference: pages 105 - 112

Raises are the easiest responses to deal with because responder is announcing that a Magic Fit has been found. There is no need to search further for an acceptable denomination in which to place the final contract . . . responder has told opener WHERE to play the hand. The only question that remains is HOW HIGH.

EXERCISE ONE: RESPONDER'S RAISE

Review Responder's First Question.

What do the following responses to an opening bid of One Heart show?

Two Hearts?   Three Hearts?   Four Hearts?

_____   _____   _____

What is the bidding message (sign-off, invitational or forcing) for each of these responses?

_____   _____   _____

WHERE is the partnership going to play the hand? What remains to be decided?

_____   _____

EXERCISE TWO: OPENER'S REBID AFTER A SINGLE RAISE

What would your opening bid be on each of the following hands?
How would you classify the strength of each hand (Minimum, Medium or Maximum)?
If responder raised your opening bid to the two-level, what rebid would you make with each hand?

1) ♠ J 9
    ♡ A Q 8 5 3
    ◇ A 5 3
    ♣ Q 9 4

2) ♠ Q 6
    ♡ K J 6 4 2
    ◇ A 2
    ♣ A Q 6 3

3) ♠ A K
    ♡ Q J 9 7 3 2
    ◇ A K 2
    ♣ Q 8

Opening: _____
Strength: _____
Rebid: _____

Opening: _____
Strength: _____
Rebid: _____

Opening: _____
Strength: _____
Rebid: _____

EXERCISE THREE: OPENER'S REBID AFTER A JUMP RAISE

What would your opening bid be on each of the following hands?
How would you classify the strength of each hand (Minimum, Medium or Maximum)?
If responder raised your opening bid to the three-level, what rebid would you make with each hand?

1) ♠ K J 7 6
   ♡ Q 8 3
   ◇ A J 6
   ♣ Q 6 3

   Opening: _____
   Strength: _____
   Rebid: _____

2) ♠ A Q 7 6 3
   ♡ 9 3
   ◇ J 4
   ♣ A K 6 3

   Opening: _____
   Strength: _____
   Rebid: _____

3) ♠ K Q 8 7 6
   ♡ A K 7 6
   ◇ K J
   ♣ 3 2

   Opening: _____
   Strength: _____
   Rebid: _____

EXERCISE FOUR: OPENER'S REBID AFTER A GAME RAISE

What would your opening bid be on each of the following hands?
How would you classify the strength of each hand (Minimum, Medium or Maximum)?
If responder raised your opening bid to the four-level, what rebid would you make with each hand?

1) ♠ J 7 6 3
   ♡ Q 9 4 2
   ◇ K 7
   ♣ A K 3

   Opening: _____
   Strength: _____
   Rebid: _____

2) ♠ A K Q 9
   ♡ Q 7 6 5 3
   ◇ Q
   ♣ K 9 8

   Opening: _____
   Strength: _____
   Rebid: _____

3) ♠ A 9 8
   ♡ A Q J 6 4 2
   ◇ A K 5
   ♣ 2

   Opening: _____
   Strength: _____
   Rebid: _____

LET'S EXPERIMENT

Construct the following hand, and place it face-up on the table:

Hand #13

```
                    ♠ Q 8 4 2
                    ♡ K 5
                    ◇ K 7 2
                    ♣ 10 7 5 3

   ♠ J 9 7                          ♠ A K
   ♡ 9 8 4 2          N            ♡ Q J 10 7 6 3
   ◇ 6 4 3         W     E         ◇ A 9 5
   ♣ A Q 8            S            ♣ K 4

                    ♠ 10 6 5 3
                    ♡ A
                    ◇ Q J 10 8
                    ♣ J 9 6 2
```

Assume that North is the dealer. Will North open the bidding? If not, who will open the bidding? What will the opening bid be?

_____   _____   _____

What bid will responder make? What will opener's rebid be? What will the final contract be?

_____   _____   _____

Who will be the opening leader? What card should he lead? What does this tell his partner?

_____   _____   _____

What problem will declarer have when he wins the opening lead? Why should declarer not lead trumps immediately?

_____   _____

Which suit should declarer play before drawing trumps? How will this help declarer make his contract?

_____   _____

Have each player pick up his hand. Start the bidding with North and complete the auction. Then play out the hand.

What are two reasons that declarer may have to delay drawing trumps when playing a hand?

_____   _____

Now construct the following hand, and place it face-up on the table:

Hand #14

```
              ♠ Q 10 2
              ♡ K 5 3
              ◇ Q 8 5 2
              ♣ K J 2

 ♠ J 7 6 3         N         ♠ 9 8 4
 ♡ Q J 4                     ♡ A 10 9 7 2
 ◇ K J 4       W       E     ◇ 10
 ♣ 9 7 4                     ♣ A 10 8 3
                   S
              ♠ A K 5
              ♡ 8 6
              ◇ A 9 7 6 3
              ♣ Q 6 5
```

Assume that East is the dealer. Will East open the bidding? If not, who will open the bidding? What will the opening bid be?

_____   _____   _____

What bid will responder make? What will opener's rebid be? What will the final contract be?

_____ _____ _____

Have each player pick up his hand. Start the bidding with East and complete the auction. Then play out the hand.

How should declarer play the Diamond suit? When can declarer afford to lead a high card rather than lead toward a high card?

_____ _____

SUMMARY

OPENER'S REBID AFTER A RAISE

After a Single Raise:	13 - 16 points	_____.
	17 - 18 points	Raise to the _____.
	19 - 21 points	Raise to the _____.
After a Jump Raise:	13 - 14 points	_____.
	15 - 21 points	Raise to the _____.
After a Game Raise:	13 - 16 points	_____.
	17 - 18 points	Raise to the _____.
	19 - 21 points	Raise to the _____.

UNIT ELEVEN: RESPONDER'S REBID AFTER OPENER'S MINIMUM REBID

Joy of Bridge reference: pages 113 - 131

Some auctions end swiftly. For example, opener bids One Heart, responder raises to Two Hearts and opener, with a minimum hand, says Pass. In many auctions, however, the final contract will not have been determined by opener's rebid. Responder's bid at this point is called responder's rebid.

EXERCISE ONE: RESPONDER ASKS HOW HIGH AND WHERE (6 - 10 POINTS)

Your partner opens the bidding One Diamond and you respond One Heart. Your partner rebids One No Trump, showing a minimum opening bid (13 - 15 points). Ask the question HOW HIGH to determine whether you want to be in Part-Game, Game or Maybe Game on each of the following hands. Then ask WHERE to help choose your best rebid.

1) ♠ K 8 7
    ♡ A 9 6 3
    ◇ J 6 4
    ♣ 9 7 4

    How High: _____
    Where: _____
    Rebid: _____

2) ♠ 7
    ♡ Q J 9 6 4
    ◇ K 9 6 5 3
    ♣ J 5

    How High: _____
    Where: _____
    Rebid: _____

3) ♠ 9 2
    ♡ K Q 8 5 4 2
    ◇ 6 2
    ♣ 8 5 3

    How High: _____
    Where: _____
    Rebid: _____

EXERCISE TWO: RESPONDER ASKS HOW HIGH AND WHERE (11 - 12 POINTS)

Your partner opens the bidding One Heart and you respond One Spade. Your partner rebids Two Hearts, showing a minimum hand (13 - 16 points).
Ask the question HOW HIGH to determine whether you want to be in Part-Game, Game or Maybe Game on each of the following hands. Then ask WHERE to help choose your best rebid.

1) ♠ K J 7 3
    ♡ A 8 7
    ◇ 9 2
    ♣ K 6 4 3

    How High: _____
    Where: _____
    Rebid: _____

2) ♠ K 10 9 4
    ♡ J 3
    ◇ Q J 8 5
    ♣ A J 4

    How High: _____
    Where: _____
    Rebid: _____

3) ♠ A K J 10 8 5
    ♡ 3
    ◇ Q 7 4
    ♣ 9 8 2

    How High: _____
    Where: _____
    Rebid: _____

EXERCISE THREE: RESPONDER ASKS HOW HIGH AND WHERE (13 - 16 POINTS)

Your partner opens the bidding One Club and you respond One Heart. Your partner rebids One No Trump, showing a minimum hand (13 - 15 points).
Ask the question HOW HIGH to determine whether you want to be in Part-Game, Game or Maybe Game on each of the following hands. Then ask WHERE to help choose your best rebid.

1) ♠ K Q 8 4
♥ A J 10 5
♦ K 9 3
♣ 8 4

How High: _____
Where: _____
Rebid: _____

2) ♠ A Q 5
♥ Q 10 9 6 4 3
♦ 5 2
♣ A 7

How High: _____
Where: _____
Rebid: _____

3) ♠ 4
♥ A K 8 7 6
♦ K Q 9 6 3
♣ 6 3

How High: _____
Where: _____
Rebid: _____

EXERCISE FOUR: TESTING IT OUT

Make up a minimum opening bid for the dealer: North, East, South and West in turn. Randomly divide the remaining cards.
Have responder use Responder's Four Questions for his first response and the questions HOW HIGH and WHERE for his second response.
Play the hand.

Turn the cards face-up and analyze the bidding using the Bidding Analysis Chart. Was a reasonable contract reached?

_____

LET'S EXPERIMENT

Construct the following hand, and place it face-up on the table:

Hand #15

```
                    ♠ A Q 6
                    ♡ 7 5
                    ◇ K Q 4 3
                    ♣ K 9 6 4
    ♠ K 10                          ♠ J 8 4 3 2
    ♡ Q 10 8 4        N             ♡ K J 2
    ◇ A 10 9 8 5    W     E         ◇ J
    ♣ J 10            S             ♣ Q 7 5 2
                    ♠ 9 7 5
                    ♡ A 9 6 3
                    ◇ 7 6 2
                    ♣ A 8 3
```

Assume that South is the dealer. Would South open the bidding? If not, who would open the bidding? What would the opening bid be?

_____   _____   _____

Assuming that East says Pass, what would South's response be?

_____

Assuming that West says Pass, what would North's (opener's) rebid be?

_____

Assuming that East says Pass, what would South's (responder's) rebid be? What will be the final contract?

_____   _____

What should the lead be? Why?

_____   _____

How many sure tricks can declarer count in the Spade suit after the opening lead? Why?

_____   _____

Have each player pick up his hand. Start the bidding with South and complete the auction. Then play out the hand.

Did declarer take enough tricks to make the contract? How can declarer give himself the best chance of taking two Diamond tricks?

_____   _____

Would it make a difference if East had started with the Ace of Diamonds? Why?

_____   _____

Now construct the following hand, and place it face-up on the table:

Hand #16

```
                      ♠ 10 9 8 7
                      ♡ 5 2
                      ◇ 9 3 2
                      ♣ K 7 5 2

      ♠ J 6 2              N              ♠ K 5 3
      ♡ A K J 4                           ♡ 10 9 8 7
      ◇ Q 8 5         W         E         ◇ A K J 6
      ♣ 9 6 4              S              ♣ A 8

                      ♠ A Q 4
                      ♡ Q 6 3
                      ◇ 10 7 4
                      ♣ Q J 10 3
```

Assume that West is the dealer. Would West open the bidding?

_____

Assuming that North says Pass, what would East's opening bid be?

_____

Assuming that South says Pass, what would West's response be?

_____

Assume that North says Pass, what would East's (opener's) rebid be? What does this tell West about opener's strength?

_____   _____

What would West's (responder's) rebid be? What does this tell East about West's strength?

_____   _____

What would East do now? Why?

_____   _____

What should the lead be? What does this tell his partner?

_____   _____

Have each player pick up his hand. Start the bidding with West and complete the auction. Then play out the hand.

Did declarer take enough tricks to make the contract? How can declarer avoid losing a trick in the trump suit?

_____   _____

SUMMARY

RESPONDER'S REBID WHEN OPENER COULD HAVE A MINIMUM HAND

Ask yourself HOW HIGH and WHERE.

With 6 - 10 points, Game is unlikely so make a discouraging rebid:

- _____.

- Bid an _____ suit at the _____.

- Bid _____.

With 11 - 12 points, Game is likely so make an encouraging rebid:

- Bid an _____ suit at the _____.

- Bid _____.

With 13 or more points, Game is certain so make sure you get there:

- Bid _____ if you know WHERE.

- Bid a _____ suit if you don't know WHERE.

UNIT TWELVE: RESPONDER'S REBID AFTER OPENER'S MEDIUM OR MAXIMUM REBID

Joy of Bridge reference: pages 132 - 146

While opener will most frequently show a minimum (13 - 16 point) hand with his rebid, there will be times when his rebid promises a medium (17 - 18 point) or maximum (19 - 21 point) hand.

Responder continues to ask the questions HOW HIGH and WHERE to help determine his appropriate rebid.

EXERCISE ONE: AFTER OPENER'S MEDIUM REBID

Your partner opens the bidding One Diamond and you respond One Heart. Your partner rebids Three Hearts showing a medium hand (17 - 18 points) and at least four Hearts. On each of the following hands ask yourself HOW HIGH and WHERE to determine the appropriate rebid as responder.

1) ♠ J 7 4
♡ Q J 8 3
◇ 9 2
♣ Q 8 7 2

How High: _____
Where: _____
Rebid: _____

2) ♠ 8 2
♡ Q J 9 7 3
◇ J 7 4
♣ A 8 3

How High: _____
Where: _____
Rebid: _____

3) ♠ K Q 7 3
♡ A J 5 4
◇ 9 8
♣ J 7 6

How High: _____
Where: _____
Rebid: _____

EXERCISE TWO: AFTER OPENER'S MAXIMUM REBID

Your partner opens the bidding One Heart and you respond One Spade. Partner rebids Three Clubs (Jump Shift) showing a maximum hand (19 - 21 points) with at least five Hearts and four Clubs.
On each of the following hands ask yourself HOW HIGH and WHERE to determine the appropriate rebid as responder.

1) ♠ J 9 7 6
♡ 5 3
◇ K J 7 4
♣ J 8 2

How High: _____
Where: _____
Rebid: _____

2) ♠ K 9 8 4
♡ K 8 3
◇ 7 5 2
♣ 8 4 2

How High: _____
Where: _____
Rebid: _____

3) ♠ A J 7 3 2
♡ 9
◇ A 9 7 4 2
♣ J 3

How High: _____
Where: _____
Rebid: _____

EXERCISE THREE: PRACTICING RESPONDER'S QUESTIONS HOW HIGH AND WHERE

In turn, give North, East, South and West opening bids that are either medium (17 - 18 points) or maximum (19 - 21 points).

Randomly divide the remaining cards among the other three players.

Have responder use Responder's Four Questions to arrive at his initial response and use the questions HOW HIGH and WHERE for his rebid.

Play the hand.

Use the Bidding Analysis Chart to determine if you got to the right contract. Ask the familiar questions: Do you have 26 combined points? Do you have a Magic Major Suit fit?

LET'S EXPERIMENT

Construct the following hand, and place it face-up on the table:

Hand #17

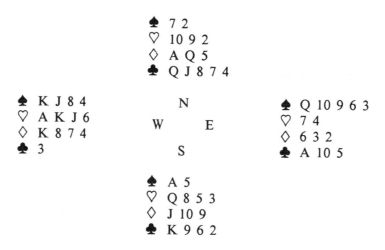

Assume that North is the dealer. What would North do? Who would open the bidding? What would the opening bid be?

——————   ——————   ——————

What would East's response be?

——————

What would West's rebid be? (Don't forget to use dummy points.)

——————

What would East's (responder's) rebid be? What would be the final contract?

——————   ——————

Have each player pick up his hand. Start the bidding with North and complete the auction. Then play out the hand.

Did declarer make his contract? What can declarer do to avoid losing two Club tricks?

——————   ——————————————

Now construct the following hand, and place it face-up on the table:

Hand #18

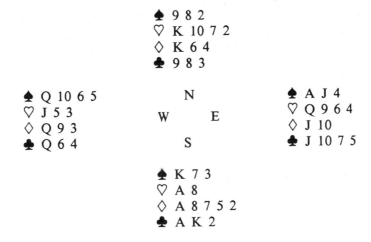

                    ♠ 9 8 2
                    ♡ K 10 7 2
                    ◇ K 6 4
                    ♣ 9 8 3

    ♠ Q 10 6 5   N   ♠ A J 4
    ♡ J 5 3   ♡ Q 9 6 4
    ◇ Q 9 3   W   E   ◇ J 10
    ♣ Q 6 4   S   ♣ J 10 7 5

                    ♠ K 7 3
                    ♡ A 8
                    ◇ A 8 7 5 2
                    ♣ A K 2

Assume that East is the dealer. Who will open the bidding? What will the opening bid be?

_____   _____

Assuming that West says Pass, what would North's response be?

_____

Assuming that East says Pass, what would South's rebid be?

_____

Assume that West says Pass, what will North do now? Why? What is the final contract?

_____   _____   _____

What should the lead be? Why?

_____   _____

Which card should the opening leader's partner lead back? Why?

_____   _____

Have each player pick up his hand. Start the bidding with East and complete the auction. Then play out the hand.

Did declarer take enough tricks to make the contract? How can declarer establish the additional tricks needed to make his contract?

_____   _____

RESPONDER'S REBID WHEN OPENER
SHOWS A MEDIUM HAND

With 6 - 8 points: Choose the best _____.

With 9 or more points: Bid _____ or make a _____ bid.

RESPONDER'S REBID WHEN OPENER
SHOWS A MAXIMUM HAND

With 6 or more points: Bid _____ or make a _____ bid.

The bidding must continue until Game is reached.

REVIEW QUESTIONS FOR BIDDING WITHOUT COMPETITION

EXERCISE ONE: OPENING THE BIDDING

What would you bid with each of the following hands?

1) ♠ A K Q J
   ♡ J 10 9 8 7
   ◇ K 3
   ♣ 6 2

   Bid: _____

2) ♠ A 8 7 4
   ♡ A Q J 2
   ◇ K 8 5
   ♣ Q J

   Bid: _____

3) ♠ K 8
   ♡ K 8 6 5 4
   ◇ A 9 7 5 3
   ♣ A

   Bid: _____

4) ♠ J 10 9
   ♡ K Q 7 6
   ◇ A Q 7 5
   ♣ Q 10

   Bid: _____

5) ♠ K J 6 3
   ♡ K Q 9 3
   ◇ 8
   ♣ A 9 7 3

   Bid: _____

6) ♠ A J 7 6 3
   ♡ Q 9 5
   ◇ Q 7 4
   ♣ J 7

   Bid: _____

EXERCISE TWO: RESPONSES TO ONE NO TRUMP

Your partner opens the bidding One No Trump. What would you respond with each of the following hands?

1) ♠ A 7 2
   ♡ A 10 9
   ◇ K 3 2
   ♣ 10 9 8 7

   Response: _____

2) ♠ 10 8 7 6 5 3
   ♡ 7 4
   ◇ Q J
   ♣ 8 7 6

   Response: _____

3) ♠ 4 3 2
   ♡ 8 7
   ◇ A K 8 7 5 3
   ♣ 7 6

   Response: _____

4) ♠ 8 2
   ♡ A Q 8 6 4 3
   ◇ K 8
   ♣ 10 6 5

   Response: _____

5) ♠ K 5
   ♡ Q 8 2
   ◇ 10 7 5 3
   ♣ 8 6 4 2

   Response: _____

6) ♠ K J 9 6 4
   ♡ A 8 2
   ◇ K 9 6
   ♣ Q 3

   Response: _____

EXERCISE THREE: RESPONSES TO OPENING BIDS AT THE ONE-LEVEL

Your partner opens the bidding One Heart. What would you respond with each of the following hands?

1) ♠ J 8 7 4
    ♡ A K
    ♢ A Q 8 6
    ♣ K 8 7

    Response: _____

2) ♠ 6
    ♡ 10 9 8 6
    ♢ Q J 10 8
    ♣ A J 10 7

    Response: _____

3) ♠ 5 3 2
    ♡ 9 8
    ♢ 10 9 7 6 4 2
    ♣ A Q

    Response: _____

4) ♠ K 9 8 6 4
    ♡ 7
    ♢ 9 7 4
    ♣ 10 8 6 3

    Response: _____

5) ♠ A 3
    ♡ J 7
    ♢ A K J 8 4
    ♣ K 9 6 4

    Response: _____

6) ♠ A J 8 6
    ♡ 9 6 5 3
    ♢ 3
    ♣ 7 5 4 2

    Response: _____

EXERCISE FOUR: MORE RESPONSES

Your partner opens the bidding One Diamond. What would you respond with each of the following hands?

1) ♠ 8 7 6 5
    ♡ 10 9
    ♢ A Q 9 7
    ♣ 7 6 3

    Response: _____

2) ♠ A K 8 6
    ♡ J 10 8 4
    ♢ 9 5
    ♣ Q 8 2

    Response: _____

3) ♠ Q 10
    ♡ J 9 7
    ♢ 7 3
    ♣ K J 9 7 4 3

    Response: _____

4) ♠ 6 3
    ♡ K 8 6
    ♢ K J 9 8
    ♣ J 7 4 2

    Response: _____

5) ♠ A J 7
    ♡ K 6
    ♢ A Q 9 7 6
    ♣ J 8 3

    Response: _____

6) ♠ 9 7
    ♡ Q 10 2
    ♢ A J 7 5 3
    ♣ K 8 4

    Response: _____

EXERCISE FIVE: OPENER'S REBID

You open the bidding One Club and your partner responds One Heart. What would you rebid with each of the following hands?

1) ♠ K J 8 5
    ♡ 9 7
    ♢ A 8 3
    ♣ A J 10 8

    Rebid: _____

2) ♠ Q 10 9
    ♡ J 7
    ♢ A Q 8
    ♣ K Q 7 6 3

    Rebid: _____

3) ♠ A 7 3
    ♡ 10 7 5 3
    ♢ K J
    ♣ K Q J 10

    Rebid: _____

4) ♠ A K 3
    ♡ 4 2
    ♢ 8 7
    ♣ A K J 9 8 4

    Rebid: _____

5) ♠ 7 5
    ♡ A 4
    ♢ A Q 8 2
    ♣ A K 7 5 3

    Rebid: _____

6) ♠ A Q 4
    ♡ K 9
    ♢ K Q 4
    ♣ A J 10 8 4

    Rebid: _____

EXERCISE SIX: OPENER'S REBID AFTER A TWO-LEVEL RESPONSE

You open the bidding One Spade and your partner responds Two Hearts. What would you rebid with each of the following hands?

1) ♠ A J 7 5 3
   ♡ J 8 5 3
   ◇ K Q
   ♣ J 3

   Rebid: _____

2) ♠ A K J 10 6
   ♡ A 9 8 4
   ◇ K 8 4
   ♣ 2

   Rebid: _____

3) ♠ A Q 9 7 5
   ♡ J 3
   ◇ Q 10 2
   ♣ K J 10

   Rebid: _____

4) ♠ K Q 10 9 3
   ♡ Q 3
   ◇ A Q 6
   ♣ K Q 10

   Rebid: _____

5) ♠ A Q J 8 7
   ♡ J 4
   ◇ 7
   ♣ A K 9 6 4

   Rebid: _____

6) ♠ A K 10 8 7 2
   ♡ 8 4
   ◇ Q 6 3
   ♣ A 5

   Rebid: _____

EXERCISE SEVEN: RESPONDER'S REBID

Your partner opens the bidding One Heart and you respond One Spade. Your partner rebids One No Trump. What would you rebid with each of the following hands?

1) ♠ J 9 8 5
   ♡ A 3
   ◇ K 9 6 4
   ♣ J 8 3

   Rebid: _____

2) ♠ A J 10 8
   ♡ K 6
   ◇ Q 9 8 3
   ♣ K J 6

   Rebid: _____

3) ♠ J 9 8 6 5 3
   ♡ 5 4
   ◇ A 7 4
   ♣ 6 3

   Rebid: _____

4) ♠ K 10 9 5
   ♡ J 8
   ◇ K 9 7
   ♣ K Q 6 4

   Rebid: _____

5) ♠ A J 9 8 6
   ♡ A 8 5
   ◇ K Q 9 7
   ♣ 4

   Rebid: _____

6) ♠ K J 10 9 7 3
   ♡ 9 2
   ◇ A 6
   ♣ Q 7 2

   Rebid: _____

EXERCISE EIGHT: RESPONDER'S REBID AFTER OPENER BIDS A NEW SUIT

Your partner opens the bidding One Heart and you respond One Spade. Your partner rebids Two Clubs. What would you rebid with each of the following hands?

1) ♠ Q J 7 5
   ♡ 5 4 2
   ◇ J 8 6 3
   ♣ Q 9

   Rebid: _____

2) ♠ K Q J 7 5 4
   ♡ 9
   ◇ J 8 4 2
   ♣ 4 2

   Rebid: _____

3) ♠ Q 9 5 3
   ♡ 3
   ◇ K 8 4 3
   ♣ Q J 9 2

   Rebid: _____

4) ♠ A Q 10 4
   ♡ J 9
   ◇ K J 8 4
   ♣ 9 7 4

   Rebid: _____

5) ♠ K 8 4 2
   ♡ A 9 3
   ◇ A 8 5
   ♣ J 10 3

   Rebid: _____

6) ♠ A J 10 7
   ♡ Q 5
   ◇ K Q 9 6
   ♣ J 9 4

   Rebid: _____

UNIT THIRTEEN: THE DOUBLE

Joy of Bridge reference: pages 144 - 146

There is a way to increase the penalty for defeating an opponent's contract. If an opponent reaches a contract which you feel cannot be made, instead of saying Pass, you can say Double when it is your turn to bid.

EXERCISE ONE: THE DOUBLE INCREASES THE PENALTY

Determine the score for defeating a contract of Three No Trump by two tricks in each of the following cases:

Not vulnerable, not doubled: _____

Not vulnerable, doubled: _____

Vulnerable, not doubled: _____

Vulnerable, doubled: _____

EXERCISE TWO: MAKING A DOUBLED PART-GAME

Determine the score for making a contract of Two Hearts in the following cases:

Not vulnerable, not doubled: _____

Not vulnerable, doubled: _____

Vulnerable, not doubled: _____

Vulnerable, doubled: _____

EXERCISE THREE: MAKING A DOUBLED GAME

Determine the score for making a contract of Four Spades in the following cases:

Not vulnerable, not doubled: _____

Not vulnerable, doubled: _____

Vulnerable, not doubled: _____

Vulnerable, doubled: _____

UNIT FOURTEEN: THE OVERCALL

Joy of Bridge reference: pages 147 - 154

Suppose you were planning to open the bidding but one of your opponents beat you to it. What can you do? One of your choices is to go ahead and bid your own suit. Since you are making a call (bid) over the opponent's bid, this is known as an overcall.

EXERCISE ONE: THE ADVANTAGES

What are some of the reasons you might want to enter the bidding after one of your opponents has opened the bidding?

_____

_____

_____

EXERCISE TWO: THE RISKS

What are some of the risks of bidding when the opponents have opened the bidding?

_____

_____

_____

EXERCISE THREE: THE OVERCALL

Your right-hand opponent opens the bidding One Diamond. What would you bid with each of the following hands?

1) ♠ A K 9 6 4
    ♡ 7 4
    ♢ A 8 3
    ♣ Q 9 4

    Bid: _____

2) ♠ Q 10 7 3
    ♡ A J 8
    ♢ K Q 9
    ♣ A J 4

    Bid: _____

3) ♠ Q 8 5 4 2
    ♡ J 9
    ♢ K Q 8 3
    ♣ 9 4

    Bid: _____

EXERCISE FOUR: PRACTICING OVERCALLS

In turn, make up an opening bid of One Club, One Diamond and One Heart for the opening bidder.

For the opening bidder's left-hand opponent make up an overcall that could be made at the one-level.

Randomly divide the remaining cards between the other two players.

Bid and play the hand. Have the partner of the opening bidder and the partner of the overcaller use Responder's Four Questions to determine their best response.

When the hand is over, use the Hand Analysis Chart to examine the bidding.

SUMMARY

REQUIREMENTS FOR MAKING AN OVERCALL

- A __-card suit or longer

- An _____ (13 - 21 points)

REQUIREMENTS FOR A ONE NO TRUMP OVERCALL

- _____ points

- _____ hand

UNIT FIFTEEN: RESPONDING TO A ONE-LEVEL OVERCALL

Joy of Bridge reference: pages 155 - 164

When you are responding to partner's overcall, treat it in the same manner as responding to an opening bid. Ask yourself Responder's Four Questions.

EXERCISE ONE: CAN I RAISE PARTNER'S MAJOR?

Your left-hand opponent opens One Diamond and your partner overcalls One Heart. Your right-hand opponent passes. What do you respond to your partner's overcall on each of the following hands? Remember to count dummy points when raising partner's major.

1) ♠ 7 4 2
♡ Q 8 6 3
◊ J 8 4
♣ 10 6 3

Dummy Points: _____
Response: _____

2) ♠ A 7 4
♡ Q 9 3
◊ J 6
♣ 8 6 5 3 2

Dummy Points: _____
Response: _____

3) ♠ K J 3
♡ K 8 6 3
◊ 8
♣ Q 9 6 5 3

Dummy Points: _____
Response: _____

EXERCISE TWO: DO I HAVE A WEAK HAND (0 - 5 POINTS)?

Your left-hand opponent opens the bidding One Club. Partner overcalls One Heart. Construct a hand that would Pass in response to your partner's overcall.

♠
♡
◊
♣

EXERCISE THREE: CAN I BID A NEW SUIT AT THE ONE-LEVEL?

Your left-hand opponent bids One Club and your partner overcalls One Heart. Your right-hand opponent passes. What do you respond to your partner's overcall on each of the following hands?

1) ♠ K Q J 8 4
♡ 9 4
◊ 8 5
♣ A 8 6 3

Response: _____

2) ♠ Q 9 6 5
♡ J 2
◊ 8 5 3
♣ 10 6 4 2

Response: _____

3) ♠ Q 10 9 7 5
♡ K 9 7
◊ 9 7
♣ K 10 8

Response: _____

EXERCISE FOUR: DO I HAVE A MINIMUM HAND (6 - 10 POINTS)?

Your left-hand opponent starts with One Club and your partner overcalls One Diamond. Your right-hand opponent says Pass. For each of the following hands, what would you respond to your partner's overcall of One Diamond?

1) ♠ Q 8 5
    ♡ Q J 7
    ◇ J 6
    ♣ Q 9 6 4 3

2) ♠ K 4 3
    ♡ J 9
    ◇ Q 8 4 3
    ♣ J 9 7 2

3) ♠ J 8 2
    ♡ K Q 3
    ◇ K Q 9 4
    ♣ K J 9

Response: _____

Response: _____

Response: _____

LET'S EXPERIMENT

Construct the following hand, and place it face-up on the table:

Hand #19

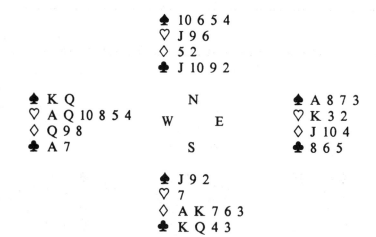

Assume that South is the dealer. Who would open the bidding? What would be the opening bid?

_____   _____

What would West do at his first opportunity?

_____

Assuming that North says Pass, what would East's response be?

_____

Assuming that South says Pass, what would West's rebid be?

_____

Assuming that North, East and South all say Pass, what is the final contract?

_____

What should the lead be? Why?

_____ _____

What should South do after winning the first trick? Why?

_____ _____

Use Declarer's Four Questions to help West decide how to plan the play of the contract.
Have each player pick up his hand. Start the bidding with South and complete the auction. Then play out the hand.

Did declarer take enough tricks to make the contract? How can declarer avoid losing a Club trick?

_____ _____

What must declarer be careful to do in order to make his contract?

_____

Now construct the following hand, and place it face-up on the table:

Hand #20

```
                     ♠ A K 3
                     ♡ A 8 2
                     ◊ K 9 4 2
                     ♣ Q 7 6

   ♠ Q J 10 8 5          N          ♠ 9 4 2
   ♡ Q J 3                          ♡ 10 7 6 4
   ◊ J 5           W       E        ◊ Q 10 8 7
   ♣ A K 2                          ♣ 9 4
                       S
                     ♠ 7 6
                     ♡ K 9 5
                     ◊ A 6 3
                     ♣ J 10 8 5 3
```

Assume that West is the dealer. Who would open the bidding? What would be the opening bid?

_____   _____

What would North do at his first opportunity?

_____

Assuming that East says Pass, what would South's response be?

_____

Assuming that West says Pass, what would North do? What is the final contract?

_____   _____

What should the lead be? Why?

_____   _____

Use Declarer's Four Questions to help North decide how to plan the play of the contract.
Have each player pick up his hand. Start the bidding with West and complete the auction. Then play out the hand.

Did declarer take enough tricks to make the contract? How can declarer establish the additional tricks needed to make his contract?

_____   _____

SUMMARY

RESPONSES TO AN OVERCALL AT THE ONE-LEVEL

1. CAN I RAISE PARTNER'S MAJOR? (You only need 3-card support.)

    If the answer is YES: Revalue your hand using _____
    points and raise to the appropriate level.

    0 - 5 points: _____.

    6 - 10 points: Raise to the _____.

    11 - 12 points: Raise to the _____.

    13 - 16 points: Raise to the _____.

2. DO I HAVE A WEAK HAND (0 - 5 POINTS)?

    If the answer is YES: _____.

3. CAN I BID A NEW SUIT AT THE ONE-LEVEL?

    If the answer is YES: Bid _____.

4. DO I HAVE A MINIMUM HAND (6 - 10 POINTS)?

    If the answer is YES: Raise opener's Minor suit to the _____
    with 3-card support.

    Bid _____.

    If the answer is NO: Raise opener's Minor suit to the _____
    with 11 - 12 points and 3-card support.

    Raise opener's Minor suit to _____
    with 13 - 16 points and 3-card support.

    Bid _____.

UNIT SIXTEEN: RESPONDING TO A TWO-LEVEL OVERCALL

Joy of Bridge reference: pages 165 - 170

When your partner makes an overcall at the two-level, you know that he has
a 5-card or longer suit and an opening bid (13 - 21 points). You can
respond as if to an opening bid except that the first bid for your side is
at the two-level. This has taken away some of your bidding room on the
Bidding Ladder. You can still use Responder's Four Questions to guide you
to the appropriate response but, since you are already at the two-level,
there will be some modifications to the answers.

EXERCISE ONE: CAN I SUPPORT PARTNER'S MAJOR?

Your left-hand opponent opens the bidding One Spade and your partner overcalls Two
Hearts. Your right-hand opponent passes and it is your bid. What do you respond to
your partner's overcall at the two-level with each of the following hands?

1) ♠ Q J 4
    ♡ 10 9 6 2
    ◇ K 7 4
    ♣ J 8 3

2) ♠ A J 8 3
    ♡ A 8 3
    ◇ 6
    ♣ 9 7 6 4 3

3) ♠ A 7 3
    ♡ K J 4
    ◇ A 8 7 4 3
    ♣ 5 2

Response: _____

Response: _____

Response: _____

EXERCISE TWO: THE NEXT THREE QUESTIONS

Your left-hand opponent opens the bidding One Spade and your partner overcalls Two
Diamonds. Your right-hand opponent passes and it is your bid. What do you do with
each of the following hands?

1) ♠ 8 7 5 4 3
    ♡ J 9 2
    ◇ 5 3
    ♣ 10 8 4

2) ♠ J 6
    ♡ K J 8 5 2
    ◇ 8 4
    ♣ Q 6 3 2

3) ♠ K J 2
    ♡ Q 9 3
    ◇ 8 5
    ♣ J 10 7 6 4

Response: _____

Response: _____

Response: _____

What would your response have been on each hand if left-hand opponent had opened One
Club and partner had overcalled *One* Diamond?

Response: _____

Response: _____

Response: _____

What effect is there on the answers to Responder's Four Questions when partner overcalls at the two-level rather than the one-level?

_____

EXERCISE THREE: THE FINAL CHOICE

Your left-hand opponent opens the bidding One Heart and your partner overcalls Two Diamonds. Your right-hand opponent passes. What do you respond with each of the following hands?

1) ♠ K Q 4
   ♡ 7 6 3
   ◊ Q J 8 6
   ♣ K 7 6

   Response: _____

2) ♠ Q 10 2
   ♡ K Q 10
   ◊ J 8 6 5
   ♣ A J 10

   Response: _____

3) ♠ A Q 9 6 5
   ♡ 9 4
   ◊ Q 7
   ♣ A 8 7 3

   Response: _____

LET'S EXPERIMENT

Construct the following hand, and place it face-up on the table:

Hand #21

```
                        ♠ A K Q 10 3
                        ♡ 7 5
                        ◊ Q 10 8
                        ♣ Q 5 4
        ♠ 9 7 5 2              N              ♠ J 6 4
        ♡ K 9 3                               ♡ A Q J 10 2
        ◊ A K 7         W            E        ◊ J 5
        ♣ K 8 3                               ♣ A J 10
                              S
                        ♠ 8
                        ♡ 8 6 4
                        ◊ 9 6 4 3 2
                        ♣ 9 7 6 2
```

Assume that North is the dealer. What would be the opening bid?

_____

What would East do at his first opportunity?

_____

Assuming that South says Pass, what would West's response be?

_____

What would North, East and South do next? What is the final contract?

_____   _____

What should the lead be? Why?

_____   _____

What should North do after winning the first trick? Why might North continue to lead Spades even though he knows that East does not have any left?

_____   _____

What must East be careful to do if North leads a Spade at trick four?

_____

Use Declarer's Four Questions to help East decide how to plan the play of the contract.
Have each player pick up his hand. Start the bidding with North and complete the auction. Then play out the hand.

Did declarer take enough tricks to make the contract? How can declarer avoid losing a Club trick?

_____   _____

Could East make the contract if South had the Queen of Clubs? Why would East expect North to hold the Queen on this hand?

_____   _____

Now construct the following hand, and place it face-up on the table:

Hand #22

```
                    ♠ K 7 5
                    ♡ 10 8 4
                    ◇ J 9 5 4
                    ♣ A K 3

   ♠ 10 9 4 2          N          ♠ Q J 8 3
   ♡ 9 2                           ♡ K Q J 7 6
   ◇ K 8          W       E        ◇ 2
   ♣ 9 8 7 4 2                     ♣ Q J 10
                    S
                    ♠ A 6
                    ♡ A 5 3
                    ◇ A Q 10 7 6 3
                    ♣ 6 5
```

Assume that East is the dealer. What would be the opening bid?

_____

What would South do at his first opportunity?

_____

Assuming that West says Pass, what would North's response be?

_____

Assuming that East says Pass, what would South do now?

_____

Which card should be led by the opening leader? Why?

_____   _____

Use Declarer's Four Questions to help South decide how to plan the play of the contract. Have each player pick up his hand. Start the bidding with East and complete the auction. Then play out the hand.

Did declarer take enough tricks to make the contract? If declarer wins the first trick with the Ace of Hearts, what can West do when he wins a trick with the King of Diamonds?

_____   _____

Should declarer win the first trick with the Ace of Hearts? What is the advantage of "holding up" with the Ace?

_____   _____

SUMMARY

RESPONSES TO AN OVERCALL AT THE TWO-LEVEL

1. CAN I RAISE PARTNER'S MAJOR? (You only need 3-card support.)

   If the answer is YES: Revalue your hand using _____
   points and raise to the appropriate level.

   0 - 10 points: _____.

   11 - 12 points: Raise to the _____.

   13 - 16 points: Raise to the _____.

2. DO I HAVE A WEAK HAND (0 - 5 POINTS)?

   If the answer is YES: _____.

3. CAN I BID A NEW SUIT AT THE ONE-LEVEL?

   The answer is always NO.

4. DO I HAVE A MINIMUM HAND (6 - 10 POINTS)?

   If the answer is YES: _____.

   If the answer is NO: Raise opener's Minor suit to the _____
   with 11 - 12 points and 3-card support.

   Raise opener's Minor suit to _____
   with 13 - 16 points and 3-card support.

   Bid _____.

UNIT SEVENTEEN: THE TAKE-OUT DOUBLE

Joy of Bridge reference: pages 171 - 177

Your right-hand opponent opens the bidding. You can't overcall because you don't have a long suit. You do, however, have 13 or more points. What can you do?

If you have an opening bid and support for the unbid suits, you can make a take-out Double. This asks your partner to bid his best suit.

EXERCISE ONE: TO DOUBLE OR NOT TO DOUBLE?

Your right-hand opponent starts the bidding with One Heart. What is your bid on each of the following hands? Remember to use dummy points when considering a take-out double.

1) ♠ K Q 7 3
♥ 5
♦ K J 8 2
♣ A 10 7 3

Bid: _____

2) ♠ Q 9 7 3
♥ 9
♦ K 10 5 2
♣ Q J 7 2

Bid: _____

3) ♠ A J 7 3
♥ -
♦ J 10 7 6
♣ K 10 9 6 2

Bid: _____

EXERCISE TWO: TO DOUBLE OR TO OVERCALL?

Your right-hand opponent starts the bidding with One Spade. Do you Pass, overcall or double with the following hands?

1) ♠ 3 2
♥ K Q J 4 2
♦ 9 3
♣ A K J 8

Bid: _____

2) ♠ A K 9 3
♥ 8 3
♦ K 7 5
♣ K J 8 4

Bid: _____

3) ♠ 9 4
♥ A Q 7 4
♦ K J 8 5
♣ A 7 3

Bid: _____

4) ♠ K Q 10
♥ A J
♦ K Q 10 9 4
♣ Q 8 4

Bid: _____

5) ♠ -
♥ A K 6 4
♦ K Q 7 4
♣ J 8 5 4 2

Bid: _____

6) ♠ A K J 9 7
♥ 3 2
♦ A 8 7 6
♣ K 3

Bid: _____

PENALTY OR TAKE-OUT?

A Double is for Take-out if neither you nor your partner has _____

and you are doubling a _____ contract.

A Double is for Penalty if either you or your partner has _____

or you are doubling a _____ contract or higher.

REQUIREMENTS FOR A TAKE-OUT DOUBLE

- Support for the _____ suits
- _____-_____ dummy points

UNIT EIGHTEEN: RESPONDING TO A TAKE-OUT DOUBLE

Joy of Bridge reference: 178 - 191

When your partner makes a take-out Double, he is saying, "Bid your best suit, partner." When you, as responder, choose the suit, WHERE has been decided. The focus is on HOW HIGH.

EXERCISE ONE: RAISING YOUR PARTNER'S SUIT

Your left-hand opponent opens the bidding One Diamond and your partner doubles. Your right-hand opponent passes. What would you bid with the following hands?

1) ♠ 10 7 5
    ♡ K Q 9 7 3
    ◇ 6 4 2
    ♣ 6 3

2) ♠ 9 6 4 3 2
    ♡ K J 7 6
    ◇ J 8
    ♣ 9 2

3) ♠ J 7 3
    ♡ 9 2
    ◇ 9 7 4
    ♣ Q 10 9 6 5

Response: _____

Response: _____

Response: _____

What do the above hands have in common?

_____

EXERCISE TWO: INVITING TO GAME

Your left-hand opponent opens the bidding One Diamond and your partner doubles. Your right-hand opponent passes. What is your bid on each of the following hands?

1) ♠ K Q 7 5 3
    ♡ 9 7 2
    ◇ J 4
    ♣ K J 4

2) ♠ 7 3
    ♡ A J 8
    ◇ 9 3
    ♣ K Q 9 7 6 3

3) ♠ J 8 4
    ♡ K 8 4
    ◇ K Q 10 3
    ♣ Q 10 7

Response: _____

Response: _____

Response: _____

What do the above hands have in common?

_____

EXERCISE THREE: RAISING TO GAME

Your left-hand opponent opens the bidding One Club and your partner doubles. Your right-hand opponent passes. What would you respond with each of the following hands?

1) ♠ A Q J 8 4
    ♡ A 8
    ◇ 10 9 3
    ♣ J 7 4

2) ♠ J 8 3
    ♡ J 9
    ◇ A J 10 6
    ♣ K Q J 4

3) ♠ A 8
    ♡ 10 9 7 5 4 2
    ◇ A 5
    ♣ K J 6

Response: _____   Response: _____   Response: _____

What do the above hands have in common?

_____

LET'S EXPERIMENT

Construct the following hand, and place it face-up on the table:

Hand #23

```
                    ♠ 10 9 8
                    ♡ A K Q 7 6
                    ◇ Q 5
                    ♣ K 7 4

    ♠ J 3                              ♠ A K 6 5
    ♡ 10 8 4          N                ♡ J 3
    ◇ A 9 6 4 3     W   E              ◇ K 8 7
    ♣ J 10 9          S                ♣ A 8 6 3

                    ♠ Q 7 4 2
                    ♡ 9 5 2
                    ◇ J 10 2
                    ♣ Q 5 2
```

Assume that South is the dealer. Who would open the bidding? What would be the opening bid?

_____   _____

What would East do at his first opportunity?

_____

Assuming that South says Pass, what would West's response be?

_____

What would North, East and South do next? What is the final contract?

_____   _____

Use Declarer's Four Questions to help West decide how to plan the play of the contract.

Have each player pick up his hand. Start the bidding with South and complete the auction. Then play out the hand.

Did declarer take enough tricks to make the contract? How can declarer avoid losing two Club tricks?

_____   _____

Now construct the following hand, and place it face-up on the table:

Hand #24

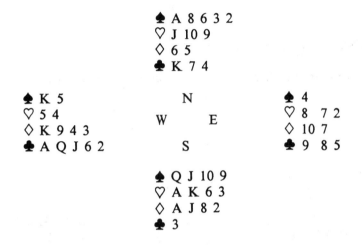

```
                      ♠ A 8 6 3 2
                      ♡ J 10 9
                      ◇ 6 5
                      ♣ K 7 4

   ♠ K 5                   N              ♠ 4
   ♡ 5 4                                  ♡ 8 7 2
   ◇ K 9 4 3         W          E         ◇ 10 7
   ♣ A Q J 6 2                            ♣ 9 8 5
                          S

                      ♠ Q J 10 9
                      ♡ A K 6 3
                      ◇ A J 8 2
                      ♣ 3
```

Assume that West is the dealer. What would be the opening bid?

_____

What would North and East do? What would South do?

_____   _____

Assuming that West says Pass, what would North's response be?

_____

Assuming that East says Pass, what would South's rebid be?

_____

Assuming that West says Pass, what would North do? What would be the final contract?

_____   _____

Use Declarer's Four Questions to help North decide how to plan the play of the contract.

Have each player pick up his hand. Start the bidding with West and complete the auction. Then play out the hand.

How can declarer avoid losing a trump trick? How can declarer avoid losing a Heart trick?

_____   _____

SUMMARY

RESPONDING TO A TAKE-OUT DOUBLE

0 - 10 points:

    Bid a 4-card or longer unbid Major suit at the _____ available level.

    Bid a 4-card or longer unbid Minor suit at the _____ available level.

    Bid _____ (rare response).

11 - 12 points:

    _____ in a 4-card or longer unbid Major suit.

    _____ in a 4-card or longer unbid Minor suit.

    _____ to Two No Trump (rare response).

13 or more points:

    Bid _____ in a 4-card or longer unbid Major suit.

    _____ to Three No Trump.

UNIT NINETEEN: THE COMPETITIVE AUCTION

Joy of Bridge reference: pages 192 - 206

We've come a long way! First we looked at bidding by opener and responder without competition. Then we looked at what to do if your opponents open the bidding. Now we'll tie it all together and see what happens when everyone is bidding.

EXERCISE ONE: PARTNER OPENS AND THERE IS AN OVERCALL AT THE ONE-LEVEL

Partner opens One Club and your right-hand opponent bids One Heart. What would you do with each of the following hands?

1) ♠ K 9 8 7 3
   ♥ A 6 2
   ♦ J 5 4
   ♣ Q 9

   Response: _____

2) ♠ Q 7 6 3
   ♥ J 8 6 5
   ♦ A 9 7 5
   ♣ 3

   Response: _____

3) ♠ Q 8 3
   ♥ K J 9
   ♦ Q 10 7 4
   ♣ 5 4 2

   Response: _____

EXERCISE TWO: PARTNER OPENS AND THERE IS AN OVERCALL AT THE TWO-LEVEL

Partner opens One Spade and your right-hand opponent bids Two Diamonds. What is your bid on each of the following hands?

1) ♠ K J 7 3
   ♥ A 9 6 2
   ♦ 7 4
   ♣ K Q 6

   Response: _____

2) ♠ Q 4 2
   ♥ K J 5
   ♦ K J 7 6
   ♣ J 8 7

   Response: _____

3) ♠ A Q 9
   ♥ 9 8 2
   ♦ 8 3
   ♣ Q 7 6 4 2

   Response: _____

EXERCISE THREE: PARTNER OPENS AND THERE IS A TAKE-OUT DOUBLE

Partner opens One Heart and your right-hand opponent doubles for take-out. What do you bid with the following hands?

1) ♠ A 8
   ♥ J 10 8 3
   ♦ Q 9 4
   ♣ 10 8 6 3

   Response: _____

2) ♠ A J 8 6 5
   ♥ 7 5
   ♦ K 10 5
   ♣ Q 8 6

   Response: _____

3) ♠ K 10 3
   ♥ 8 7
   ♦ K 9 5 2
   ♣ J 7 5 4

   Response: _____

EXERCISE FOUR: PARTNER OVERCALLS AND RIGHT-HAND OPPONENT BIDS

Your left-hand opponent bids One Heart and partner bids One Spade. Your right-hand opponent raises to Two Hearts. What would you bid with each of the following hands?

1) ♠ K 7 3
    ♡ 10 2
    ◊ A 9 8 6 4
    ♣ J 8 5

2) ♠ K J 7 4
    ♡ 9 7
    ◊ A 10 7 3
    ♣ K 8 4

3) ♠ J 5
    ♡ K 10 4
    ◊ J 9 8 2
    ♣ Q 9 7 4

Response: _____

Response: _____

Response: _____

EXERCISE FIVE: PARTNER TAKE-OUT DOUBLES AND RIGHT-HAND OPPONENT BIDS

Your left-hand opponent starts with One Heart, partner doubles and your right-hand opponent bids Two Hearts. What would you bid with each of the following hands?

1) ♠ 9 7 5 3
    ♡ 6 5 3
    ◊ 10 5
    ♣ 10 7 5 3

2) ♠ A J 8 6 5
    ♡ 7 5
    ◊ 10 9 4
    ♣ Q 5 4

3) ♠ A J 10 6 3
    ♡ 9 4
    ◊ K 7 3
    ♣ Q 8 4

Response: _____

Response: _____

Response: _____

EXERCISE SIX: PUTTING IT ALL TOGETHER

Now you should be able to handle all of the bidding sequences. Have North, East, South and West deal out the cards in turn. Bid and play each hand.

Use the Hand Analysis Chart for each hand to determine if an appropriate contract was reached.

LET'S EXPERIMENT

Construct the following hand, and place it face-up on the table:

Hand #25

```
                        ♠ J 9 8 4
                        ♡ 10
                        ◊ J 8 7 4 2
                        ♣ Q 7 6

        ♠ 10 2              N            ♠ Q 5
        ♡ A K 7 6                        ♡ Q J 9 8 4 2
        ◊ A 6 3         W       E        ◊ K 5
        ♣ A J 10 9                       ♣ 4 3 2
                           S
                        ♠ A K 7 6 3
                        ♡ 5 3
                        ◊ Q 10 9
                        ♣ K 8 5
```

Assume that North is the dealer. Who would open the bidding? What would be the opening bid?

_____   _____

- 74 -

What would West do? What would North do? What would East do?

_____   _____   _____

Assuming that South says Pass, what would West's rebid be?

_____

What would North, East and South do next? What is the final contract?

_____   _____

What should South do after winning the first two tricks? Why should South not play another Spade?

_____   _____

Use Declarer's Four Questions to help East decide how to plan the play of the contract.

Have each player pick up his hand. Start the bidding with North and complete the auction. Then play out the hand.

Did declarer take enough tricks to make the contract? How can declarer get two Club tricks?

_____   _____

Now construct the following hand, and place it face-up on the table:

Hand #26

```
              ♠ 9 4 3 2
              ♡ A Q 4
              ♢ 2
              ♣ K Q J 9 8

♠ K J 8 7 6        N        ♠ Q 5
♡ J                        ♡ 10 9 8 7 6
♢ K J 6 5      W     E      ♢ 10 9 4 3
♣ A 5 4            S        ♣ 7 6

              ♠ A 10
              ♡ K 5 3 2
              ♢ A Q 8 7
              ♣ 10 3 2
```

Assume that East is the dealer. Who would open the bidding? What would be the opening bid?

_____   _____

What would West bid? What would North do? What would East do?

_____   _____   _____

What would South rebid? What would West do? What would North do?

_____   _____   _____

What would be the final contract?

_____

What should the lead be? Why?

_____   _____

Use Declarer's Four Questions to help South decide how to plan the play of the contract. Have each player pick up his hand. Start the bidding with East and complete the auction. Then play out the hand.

Did declarer take enough tricks to make the contract? Should declarer win the first trick with the Ace of Spades? What will happen if declarer doesn't win the first trick?

_____   _____   _____

SUMMARY

COMPETITIVE AUCTIONS

When responding to partner's opening bid or overcall, continue to use Responder's Four Questions even if your right-hand opponent interferes.

RESPONDER'S FOUR QUESTIONS

1. _____

2. _____

3. _____

4. _____

If the opponent's bid has interfered with your normal response, try to find a suitable substitute. With 6 - 10 points, you may Pass if you have no suitable bid. With 11 or more points, you must bid something.

When an opponent bids after your partner has made a take-out Double:

    0 - 5 points: _____ .

    6 - 10 points: _____ an unbid suit or, rarely, bid One No Trump.

    11 - 12 points: _____ in an unbid suit or, rarely, bid Two No Trump.

    13 or more points: Bid _____ .

When an opponent makes a take-out Double of your partner's opening bid, respond exactly as you would have if the opponent had said Pass.

REVIEW QUESTIONS FOR BIDDING WITH COMPETITION

EXERCISE ONE: MAKING AN OVERCALL

Your right-hand opponent opens the bidding One Heart. What do you bid on the following hands?

1) ♠ A Q J 8 6 5
   ♡ 4 3
   ◇ K 8
   ♣ Q 4 3

   Bid: _____

2) ♠ K 6
   ♡ A Q 6
   ◇ K J 9 7 5
   ♣ Q J 5

   Bid: _____

3) ♠ K J 7 6 3
   ♡ Q J 3
   ◇ K 9 3
   ♣ 8 2

   Bid: _____

4) ♠ A 9 7 5
   ♡ Q 4
   ◇ 7
   ♣ K Q J 10 8 4

   Bid: _____

5) ♠ 6 5
   ♡ 7
   ◇ A Q 9 8 6
   ♣ A K J 8 5

   Bid: _____

6) ♠ J 8
   ♡ A Q J 8
   ◇ A 8 7 4
   ♣ J 7 3

   Bid: _____

EXERCISE TWO: RESPONDING TO AN OVERCALL

Your left-hand opponent opens the bidding One Club. Your partner overcalls One Heart and your right-hand opponent says Pass. What do you bid with each of the following hands?

1) ♠ J 10 8 7 6
   ♡ 3
   ◇ Q 10 8 7 6
   ♣ 4 2

   Response: _____

2) ♠ A J 8 7
   ♡ Q 9 7 6
   ◇ 7 6
   ♣ J 8 3

   Response: _____

3) ♠ Q J 8 6 5
   ♡ 9 7
   ◇ A J 8 6
   ♣ 7 3

   Response: _____

4) ♠ K 10 4
   ♡ J 6
   ◇ Q 10 7 6
   ♣ Q J 9 7

   Response: _____

5) ♠ A 8
   ♡ 5
   ◇ A K 10 8 7 5
   ♣ Q 8 6 4

   Response: _____

6) ♠ K 9 7
   ♡ A J 7
   ◇ A J 10 7 4
   ♣ 8 4

   Response: _____

EXERCISE THREE: MAKING A TAKE-OUT DOUBLE

Your right-hand opponent opens the bidding One Spade. What do you bid with each of the following hands?

1) ♠ 8
   ♡ A J 7 5
   ◇ K Q 9 6
   ♣ K 8 7 2

   Bid: _____

2) ♠ K 9 7 6
   ♡ A 3
   ◇ K 7 6 5
   ♣ K 4 2

   Bid: _____

3) ♠ 8 3
   ♡ A K 9 7 6
   ◇ A 10
   ♣ Q J 8 7

   Bid: _____

4) ♠ -
   ♡ K Q 8 7
   ◇ J 9 8 6 5
   ♣ A 8 6 4

   Bid: _____

5) ♠ K J 5
   ♡ A J
   ◇ K 10 7 3
   ♣ A 10 9 2

   Bid: _____

6) ♠ 4 3
   ♡ A K 5 3
   ◇ K 8 7
   ♣ A J 7 6

   Bid: _____

EXERCISE FOUR: RESPONDING TO A TAKE-OUT DOUBLE

Your left-hand opponent opens the bidding One Heart, your partner says Double and your right-hand opponent says Pass. What do you bid on each of the following hands?

1) ♠ 9 7
   ♡ J 8 7
   ◇ 10 9 6
   ♣ J 8 6 5 3

   Response: _____

2) ♠ Q 10 8 7
   ♡ 8 5
   ◇ J 9 7 6 4
   ♣ K 6

   Response: _____

3) ♠ K 9 8 6 4
   ♡ 10 4
   ◇ A Q J 5
   ♣ 6 2

   Response: _____

4) ♠ A J 10 8 4
   ♡ 9 4
   ◇ 3
   ♣ K Q J 7 4

   Response: _____

5) ♠ K 4
   ♡ A J 10 3
   ◇ K 10 9
   ♣ Q 10 8 4

   Response: _____

6) ♠ K 8 5
   ♡ Q 9 5
   ◇ A J 10 8 6 3
   ♣ 4

   Response: _____

EXERCISE FIVE: MORE COMPETITIVE AUCTIONS

Your left-hand opponent opens the bidding One Diamond, your partner says Double and your right-hand opponent bids Two Diamonds. What do you bid on the following hands?

1) ♠ J 9 7 5
   ♡ 10 8 4
   ◇ Q 9 5
   ♣ J 6 5

   Response: _____

2) ♠ K Q 10 6
   ♡ A 8 4
   ◇ 10 8
   ♣ 10 6 4 2

   Response: _____

3) ♠ A 8
   ♡ A J 7 6 5 2
   ◇ 8 7 4
   ♣ Q 3

   Response: _____

4) ♠ K 10 9 6 5
   ♡ K Q 3
   ◇ 7 5 3
   ♣ K 6

   Response: _____

5) ♠ K 6 4
   ♡ Q 8 6
   ◇ A J 9 4
   ♣ J 10 3

   Response: _____

6) ♠ J 6 3
   ♡ K 6 3
   ◇ A Q 3
   ♣ K J 7 5

   Response: _____

UNIT TWENTY: THE STAYMAN CONVENTION

Joy of Bridge reference: pages 208 - 216

The Stayman Convention can be used by responder after an opening bid of
One No Trump. It uses a response of Two Clubs to discover whether or not
opener has a 4-card Major.

EXERCISE ONE: WHEN TO USE STAYMAN

Your partner opens One No Trump. On each of the following hands, do you have a
Magic Fit (yes, no or maybe)? What response do you make?

1) ♠ Q J 9 7 6 3
♥ A 8 3
♦ K 4
♣ 6 5

Magic Fit: _____
Response: _____

2) ♠ 7 2
♥ 10 9
♦ A Q 9 6
♣ K J 8 6 2

Magic Fit: _____
Response: _____

3) ♠ A Q 8 4
♥ 9 3
♦ Q 10 8 5 2
♣ J 5

Magic Fit: _____
Response: _____

4) ♠ 9
♥ K Q 7 6
♦ A J 6 4
♣ K 10 6 2

Magic Fit: _____
Response: _____

5) ♠ 7 5
♥ K J 9 6 2
♦ Q 7 4
♣ A 8 2

Magic Fit: _____
Response: _____

6) ♠ J 9 6 3
♥ A 10 8 4
♦ 5 2
♣ A J 6

Magic Fit: _____
Response: _____

EXERCISE TWO: REBIDS BY THE OPENING ONE NO TRUMP BIDDER

You open the bidding One No Trump and your partner responds Two Clubs, the
Stayman Convention. What would you rebid with each of the following hands?

1) ♠ K J 7
♥ A 9 6 3
♦ A J 7
♣ K J 8

Rebid: _____

2) ♠ J 8 7 3
♥ K Q
♦ A Q J 6
♣ Q J 5

Rebid: _____

3) ♠ A J 4
♥ K Q 6
♦ 10 2
♣ A Q 8 7 3

Rebid: _____

EXERCISE THREE: RESPONDER'S REBID WITH 10 OR MORE POINTS

Your partner opens the bidding One No Trump and you respond Two Clubs, the Stayman Convention. Your partner rebids Two Hearts. What do you do with each of the following hands?

1) ♠ A 6
♡ K 9 4 2
◇ A J 7 5 3
♣ 8 2

Rebid: _____

2) ♠ Q 10 7 3
♡ 8 2
◇ K Q 2
♣ A 10 5 2

Rebid: _____

3) ♠ A K 10 2
♡ Q 9 6 4
◇ 8 6
♣ J 7 3

Rebid: _____

EXERCISE FOUR: RESPONDER'S REBID WITH 8 - 9 POINTS

Your partner opens the bidding One No Trump and you respond Two Clubs, the Stayman Convention. Your partner rebids Two Spades. What do you do with each of the following hands?

1) ♠ K 7 6 3
♡ 9 5
◇ K 8 5 2
♣ Q 10 3

Rebid: _____

2) ♠ J 7 4
♡ A 9 8 3
◇ Q 2
♣ Q 8 6 3

Rebid: _____

3) ♠ K 8
♡ K Q 10 6 5
◇ 10 8
♣ 9 6 3 2

Rebid: _____

LET'S EXPERIMENT

Construct the following hand, and place it face-up on the table:

Hand #27

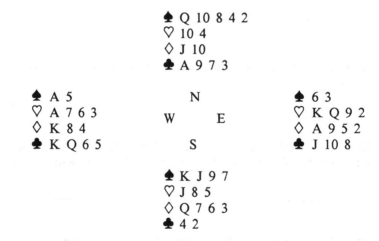

Assume that South is the dealer. Who would open the bidding? What would be the opening bid?

_____   _____

Assuming that North and South Pass throughout the auction, what would East respond? What would West rebid? What would East rebid? What would be the final contract?

——————   ——————   ——————   ——————

Use Declarer's Four Questions to help West decide how to plan the play of the contract.

Have each player pick up his hand. Start the bidding with South and complete the auction. Then play out the hand.

Did declarer take enough tricks to make the contract? What would have happened if East and West ended up in a contract of Three No Trump?

——————   ——————————————————————

Now construct the following hand, and place it face-up on the table:

Hand #28

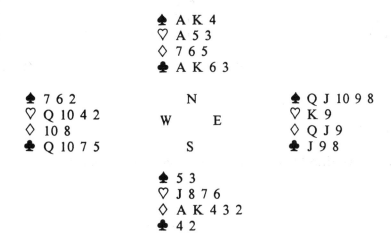

♠ A K 4
♡ A 5 3
◇ 7 6 5
♣ A K 6 3

♠ 7 6 2   N   ♠ Q J 10 9 8
♡ Q 10 4 2   W   E   ♡ K 9
◇ 10 8   ◇ Q J 9
♣ Q 10 7 5   S   ♣ J 9 8

♠ 5 3
♡ J 8 7 6
◇ A K 4 3 2
♣ 4 2

Assume that West is the dealer. Who would open the bidding? What would be the opening bid?

——————   ——————

Assuming that East and West Pass throughout the auction, what would South respond? What would North rebid? What would South rebid? What would North do?

——————   ——————   ——————   ——————

What would be the final contract? What would be the opening lead?

——————   ——————

Use Declarer's Four Questions to help North decide how to plan the play of the contract.

Have each player pick up his hand. Start the bidding with West and complete the auction. Then play out the hand.

Did declarer take enough tricks to make the contract? Which suit should declarer play to establish the additional tricks he needs?

_____   _____

What problem does declarer encounter if he takes the Ace and King of Diamonds before giving up a Diamond trick to the opponents? How can declarer overcome this problem?

_____   _____

SUMMARY

OPENER'S REBID AFTER A
TWO-CLUB (STAYMAN) RESPONSE

- _____ :   4-card (or longer) Heart suit

- _____ :   4-card (or longer) Spade suit

- _____ :   No 4-card Major

UNIT TWENTY-ONE: POWERHOUSE HANDS

Joy of Bridge reference: pages 217 - 229

Strong hands of 22 or more points are opened at the two-level. An opening bid at the two-level is called a strong two-bid. This is a signal to responder that opener has a very strong hand and, at the same time, leaves sufficient room to explore for the best Game and the possibility of Slam.

EXERCISE ONE: STRONG OPENING BIDS

How would you open the bidding with each of the following hands?

1) ♠ A K J
   ♡ A Q J
   ◇ K Q 9 4
   ♣ K J 10

   Bid: _____

2) ♠ A Q 9 8 7
   ♡ A K Q 7 3
   ◇ A
   ♣ K 4

   Bid: _____

3) ♠ 10
   ♡ A 9 6
   ◇ A K Q J 9 6 2
   ♣ A K

   Bid: _____

EXERCISE TWO: RESPONDING TO AN OPENING TWO NO TRUMP BID

Your partner opens the bidding Two No Trump. What do you respond with each of the following hands?

1) ♠ 8 4
   ♡ 9 7
   ◇ 7 5 4 3 2
   ♣ Q J 8 6

   Response: _____

2) ♠ J
   ♡ Q 9 7 5 4 2
   ◇ 9 8 6
   ♣ J 7 2

   Response: _____

3) ♠ K J 7 3
   ♡ 9 3
   ◇ K 8 7
   ♣ 10 9 8 3

   Response: _____

EXERCISE THREE: RESPONDING TO A STRONG OPENING OF TWO IN A SUIT

Your partner opens the bidding Two Spades. What do you respond with the following hands?

1) ♠ 10 7 6 3
   ♡ K J 8 4
   ◇ A 7
   ♣ 8 6 3

   Response: _____

2) ♠ 10 7
   ♡ Q J 8 6 4 3
   ◇ 9 5 2
   ♣ 8 3

   Response: _____

3) ♠ 10
   ♡ Q 9 3
   ◇ Q 8 6 5
   ♣ A J 7 6 4

   Response: _____

Construct the following hand, and place it face-up on the table:

Hand #29

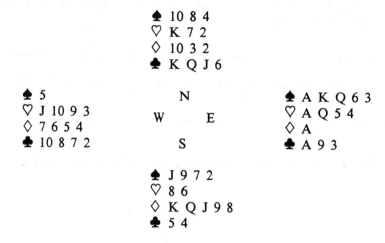

Assume that North is the dealer. Who would open the bidding? What would be the opening bid?

———————   ———————

Assuming that North and South Pass throughout the auction, what would West respond? Why?

———————   ————————————————————————————

What would East rebid? Why?

———————   ————————————————————————————

What would West rebid? Why can't West Pass?

———————   ————————————————————————————

What would East do now? Why?

———————   ————————————————————————————

Use Declarer's Four Questions to help East decide how to plan the play of the contract.

Have each player pick up his hand. Start the bidding with North and complete the auction. Then play out the hand.

Did declarer take enough tricks to make the contract? How can declarer avoid losing a trump trick?

———————   ————————————————————————————

How can declarer get to dummy? Which Heart should he lead from dummy? Why?

_____   _____   _____

Should declarer take the Ace, King and Queen of Spades before trumping a Spade in dummy? If not, why not?

_____   _____

Why does declarer only need to trump one of his little Spades in dummy?

_____

Now construct the following hand, and place it face-up on the table:

Hand #30

```
                        ♠ J 10 7 6 5 3
                        ♡ 7 4 2
                        ◇ J 6
                        ♣ 5 2

         ♠ 8 4                N              ♠ 9 2
         ♡ A 9 6 5                            ♡ Q J 10
         ◇ K 10 9 4       W         E         ◇ Q 8 7 3 2
         ♣ Q 10 4                            ♣ J 9 8
                             S
                        ♠ A K Q
                        ♡ K 8 3
                        ◇ A 5
                        ♣ A K 7 6 3
```

Assume that East is the dealer. Who would open the bidding? What would be the opening bid?

_____   _____

What would West bid? What would North do? What would East do?

_____   _____   _____

What would South do? Why?

_____   _____

What would be the final contract?

_____

Which card should be led by the opening leader? Why?

_____   _____

Use Declarer's Four Questions to help North decide how to plan the play of the contract.

Have each player pick up his hand. Start the bidding with East and complete the auction. Then play out the hand.

Did declarer take enough tricks to make the contract? How can declarer avoid losing a Diamond trick?

_____   _____

How can declarer establish the Club suit?

_____

Could declarer have made the contract if the opponents' Clubs were divided four-two? How?

_____   _____

SUMMARY

RULE FOR A TWO NO TRUMP OPENING BID

To open the bidding Two No Trump you need a

_____ hand **and** _____ points.

RULE FOR A THREE NO TRUMP OPENING BID

To open the bidding Three No Trump you need a

_____ hand **and** _____ points.

RULE FOR OPENING THE BIDDING TWO OF A SUIT

With an unbalanced hand of ____ or more points,

open the bidding at the _____ in your longest suit.

With two 5-card or 6-card suits, open the _____ suit.

With three 4-card suits, open the _____ suit.

RESPONSES TO AN OPENING BID OF TWO NO TRUMP

With 0 - 2 points: _____.

With 3 - 8 points: Bid _____ or _____ with
a 6-card or longer Major suit.

Bid _____ or _____ with
a 5-card Major suit.

Bid _____ (Stayman) with
a 4-card Major suit.

Otherwise, bid _____.

RESPONDER'S QUESTIONS AFTER AN OPENING TWO-BID

1. _____

2. _____

UNIT TWENTY-TWO: SLAM BIDDING

Joy of Bridge reference: pages 230 - 241

In addition to the Game bonus, a considerable bonus is awarded for bidding a Small Slam (six-level contract) or a Grand Slam (seven-level contract).

There is a risk associated with moving beyond the Game level in search of the big bonus for a Slam contract. You can minimize the risk and still take advantage of the opportunities to get a big bonus by using the familiar tools, HOW HIGH and WHERE.

EXERCISE ONE: HOW HIGH

Your partner opens the bidding One No Trump. HOW HIGH should you be with each of the following hands (Game, Slam or Maybe Slam)?

1) ♠ K J 10 8 6 4
   ♡ 9
   ◇ A 8
   ♣ A K 5 2

   How High: _____

2) ♠ 9 4
   ♡ A Q 10 8 6 3
   ◇ A Q 6
   ♣ 7 5

   How High: _____

3) ♠ K Q J 9 7 6
   ♡ 7
   ◇ K 9 4
   ♣ A J 8

   How High: _____

EXERCISE TWO: USING HOW HIGH AND WHERE

Your partner opens the bidding One Heart. What should you respond with each of the following hands?

1) ♠ A J 8
   ♡ A Q J 8 7
   ◇ A 9 3
   ♣ K 10

   Response: _____

2) ♠ A Q
   ♡ K J 10 4
   ◇ A 9 8 6
   ♣ K 8 5

   Response: _____

3) ♠ -
   ♡ A Q 8 7 3
   ◇ A K Q 9 5
   ♣ A J 3

   Response: _____

4) ♠ K 4
   ♡ K 9 8 7
   ◇ K Q 5
   ♣ A 8 7 5

   Response: _____

5) ♠ A K 9 8 3
   ♡ A K 3
   ◇ 6
   ♣ A J 10 8

   Response: _____

6) ♠ A K 8 4
   ♡ K Q 7 2
   ◇ A J 7 4
   ♣ 5

   Response: _____

EXERCISE THREE: RESPONDING TO A SLAM INVITATION

You open the bidding One No Trump and your partner invites you to bid a Slam by responding Four No Trump. What do you bid on each of the following hands?

1) ♠ K J 9
   ♡ Q 7
   ◇ A K 9 6
   ♣ K 7 5 3

   Rebid: _____

2) ♠ A K
   ♡ Q J 9 7
   ◇ Q 8 6 3
   ♣ K Q 9

   Rebid: _____

3) ♠ K J
   ♡ Q 9 6
   ◇ K Q 7 5 3
   ♣ A Q 10

   Rebid: _____

EXERCISE FOUR: OPENER LOOKS FOR SLAM

You open the bidding One Spade and your partner raises you to Four Spades. What do you rebid with each of the following hands?

1) ♠ A Q 9 7 5
   ♡ A
   ◇ K J 10 7 3
   ♣ A 4

   Rebid: _____

2) ♠ Q J 9 6 4
   ♡ A K
   ◇ A J 8 4
   ♣ Q 4

   Rebid: _____

3) ♠ K J 9 6 3 2
   ♡ Q J 3
   ◇ A Q J
   ♣ 3

   Rebid: _____

LET'S EXPERIMENT

Construct the following hand, and place it face-up on the table:

Hand #31

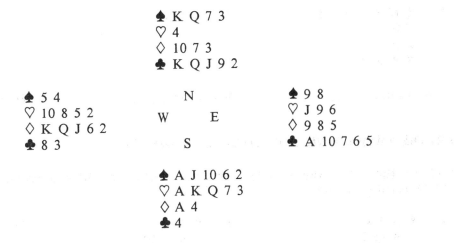

Assume that South is the dealer. What would be the opening bid?

_____

Assuming that East and West Pass throughout the auction, what would North respond? What would South do now? What would be the final contract?

_____   _____   _____

Use Declarer's Four Questions to help South decide how to plan the play of the contract. Have each player pick up his hand. Start the bidding with South and complete the auction. Then play out the hand.

Did declarer take enough tricks to make the contract? What danger is there in trying to establish tricks in the Club suit after drawing trump?

_____   _____

How can declarer avoid losing both a Club trick and a Diamond trick?

_____

Now construct the following hand, and place it face-up on the table:

Hand #32

```
                        ♠ J 10 9 8 2
                        ♡ 6 4 2
                        ◇ 8 3
                        ♣ 7 5 4

        ♠ A K 7              N              ♠ Q 4 3
        ♡ K Q J                             ♡ A 7 5
        ◇ A Q 6         W         E         ◇ K 9 2
        ♣ K Q 9 3                           ♣ J 10 6 2
                             S
                        ♠ 6 5
                        ♡ 10 9 8 3
                        ◇ J 10 7 5 4
                        ♣ A 8
```

Assume that West is the dealer. What would be the opening bid?

_____

Assuming that North and South Pass throughout the auction, what would East respond? What would West do? What would be the final contract?

_____   _____   _____

Use Declarer's Four Questions to help West decide how to plan the play of the contract. Have each player pick up his hand. Start the bidding with West and complete the auction. Then play out the hand.

Did declarer take enough tricks to make the contract? Which suit should declarer play to establish the additional tricks he needs?

_____   _____

SUMMARY

THE SLAM DECISIONS

HOW HIGH: ____ or more combined points are needed for a Small Slam.

____ or more combined points are needed for a Grand Slam.

WHERE: Play Slam in _____ Magic Fit, otherwise in No Trump.

UNIT TWENTY-THREE: PRE-EMPTIVE OPENING BIDS

Joy of Bridge reference: pages 242-257

One of the best opportunities you have to interfere with the opponents occurs when you have an opportunity to open the bidding. While you use the one-level for opening bids with 13 to 21 points and the two-level for opening bids of 22 or more points, there is nothing to stop you from opening the bidding at the three-level or higher in a suit.

EXERCISE ONE: THE OPENING BID

You are dealer and have an opportunity to open the bidding. What would you do on each of the following hands?

1)	♠ 10 6	2)	♠ A K 10 9 6 5 3	3)	♠ 9 3
	♡ 8 6		♡ 7		♡ K Q J 10 7 4 3 2
	◇ 4 3		◇ A 8 4		◇ 10 5
	♣ A Q J 8 5 3 2		♣ 9 3		♣ 10

Bid: _____   Bid: _____   Bid: _____

EXERCISE TWO: RESPONDING TO A THREE-LEVEL PRE-EMPT

Your partner opens the bidding Three Clubs. What do you bid with the following hands?

1)	♠ K Q 6 4	2)	♠ A K 8 7	3)	♠ A Q 8
	♡ K 9 8 5 3		♡ A K J 10 4 3		♡ K J 9 7
	◇ A J 5		◇ 9		◇ K 10 4 3
	♣ 5		♣ J 8		♣ A 9

Response: _____   Response: _____   Response: _____

EXERCISE THREE: REBIDS BY THE PRE-EMPTIVE OPENER

You open the bidding Three Clubs and your partner responds Three Hearts. What do you rebid with each of the following hands?

1)	♠ 10 5	2)	♠ J 9 4	3)	♠ 3
	♡ 9 6 4		♡ 5		♡ 6 4 3
	◇ 4		◇ 6 3		◇ 9 5
	♣ K J 10 8 7 6 5		♣ A Q J 9 7 6 4		♣ A K 10 7 5 4 3

Bid: _____   Bid: _____   Bid: _____

EXERCISE FOUR: BIDDING OVER AN OPPONENT'S PRE-EMPT

Your right-hand opponent opens the bidding Three Diamonds. What would you do with the following hands?

1)   ♠ A 8 7   2)   ♠ Q 8   3)   ♠ A J 5 3
     ♡ K 4   ♡ A Q J 8 6 3   ♡ K J 10 6
     ♢ Q 8 6 3   ♢ 5   ♢ 3
     ♣ K J 6 3   ♣ A J 9 8   ♣ K Q 9 7

Bid: _____   Bid: _____   Bid: _____

LET'S EXPERIMENT

Construct the following hand, and place it face-up on the table:

Hand #33

```
                    ♠ 4
                    ♡ 7 5
                    ♢ K Q J 10 6 5 3
                    ♣ 9 3 2

       ♠ A 9 8 6            N            ♠ Q J 10 2
       ♡ Q 10 6 2                        ♡ K J 4
       ♢ A 7        W            E       ♢ 9 8 2
       ♣ 10 8 7                          ♣ K Q J
                            S
                    ♠ K 7 5 3
                    ♡ A 9 8 3
                    ♢ 4
                    ♣ A 6 5 4
```

Assume that North is the dealer. What would be the opening bid?

_____

What would East do? What would South do? What would West do? What is the final contract?

_____   _____   _____   _____

Use Declarer's Four Questions to help North decide how to plan the play of the contract.

Have each player pick up his hand. Start the bidding with North and complete the auction. Then play out the hand.

Did declarer take enough tricks to make the contract? If declarer did not make the contract, was this a poor result on the hand?

_____   _____

What would have happened if North had passed instead of opening with a pre-empt?

_____

Now construct the following hand, and place it face-up on the table:

Hand #34

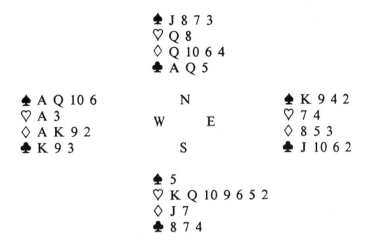

♠ J 8 7 3
♡ Q 8
◇ Q 10 6 4
♣ A Q 5

♠ A Q 10 6
♡ A 3
◇ A K 9 2
♣ K 9 3

N
W   E
S

♠ K 9 4 2
♡ 7 4
◇ 8 5 3
♣ J 10 6 2

♠ 5
♡ K Q 10 9 6 5 2
◇ J 7
♣ 8 7 4

Assume that East is the dealer. Who would open the bidding? What would be the opening bid?

——————   ——————

What would West bid? What would North do? What would East do?

——————   ——————   ——————

What would South do? What would West do?

——————   ———————————————————————

What would be the final contract? Was the pre-emptive opening bid successful?

——————   ———————————————————————

Use Declarer's Four Questions to help East decide how to plan the play of the contract. Not all contracts can be made but East should endeavour to win as many tricks as possible.

Have each player pick up his hand. Start the bidding with East and complete the auction. Then play out the hand.

Did declarer take enough tricks to make the contract? Should East and West be discouraged if they reached an unmakeable contract?

——————   ———————————————————————

What would have happened if South had not opened with a pre-empt?

———————————————————————————————————

Would East have done better to Pass West's take-out Double? If not, why not?

——————   ———————————————————————

REQUIREMENTS FOR A PRE-EMPTIVE OPENING BID

A GOOD SUIT: At least ____ of the 5 highest cards in the suit

A LONG SUIT: At least a ____-card suit

        - With a 7-card suit, open at the _____-level.

        - With an 8-card suit, open at the _____-level.

        - With a 9-card suit or longer, open at the _____-level.

A WEAK HAND: ____-____ points

RESPONDING TO A THREE-LEVEL PRE-EMPTIVE OPENING BID

0 - 15 points: _____.

16 or more points: Raise partner's Major to _____ (even with a singleton).

          Bid Four Hearts or Four Spades with a 7-card or longer suit.

          Bid Three Hearts or Three Spades with a 5- or 6-card suit.

          Bid _____.

REBIDS BY THE PRE-EMPTIVE OPENER

If responder bids at the Game level: _____.

If responder bids a new suit at the three-level:

    - _____ with 3-card support.

    - Bid _____ otherwise.

BIDDING OVER AN OPPONENT'S PRE-EMPTIVE OPENING BID

0 - 15 points: _____.

16 - 21 points: _____ with a 5-card suit or longer.

           _____ with support for the unbid suits.

          Overall _____.

22 or more points: Cue bid the opponent's suit (Marathon bid).

REVIEW QUESTIONS FOR MORE ON BIDDING

EXERCISE ONE: THE STAYMAN CONVENTION

Your partner opens the bidding One No Trump. What do you respond with each of the following hands?

1) ♠ K J 8 5
    ♡ Q 10 9 7
    ♢ A 8 3
    ♣ 6 3

    Response: _____

2) ♠ A Q 9 7 6
    ♡ J 7
    ♢ 10 9
    ♣ K 8 6 3

    Response: _____

3) ♠ J 7 3
    ♡ A J 8 7 6
    ♢ Q 9 7
    ♣ 10 2

    Response: _____

4) ♠ J 10 7 6
    ♡ K 9 7 4
    ♢ 10 5
    ♣ J 8 6

    Response: _____

5) ♠ A 10 8 7
    ♡ K 3
    ♢ A 10 9 3
    ♣ Q 7 6

    Response: _____

6) ♠ 5 4
    ♡ K J 8 6
    ♢ 8 7
    ♣ A 9 8 6 4

    Response: _____

EXERCISE TWO: RESPONDING TO STAYMAN

You open the bidding One No Trump and your partner responds Two Clubs. What do you rebid with each of the following hands?

1) ♠ A Q 10 3
    ♡ A 4
    ♢ K 10 9 4
    ♣ K J 4

    Response: _____

2) ♠ K 9 6
    ♡ J 10 8 6
    ♢ A Q J 4
    ♣ K Q

    Response: _____

3) ♠ A K 10
    ♡ A J 9
    ♢ 7 3
    ♣ K J 8 7 5

    Response: _____

4) ♠ A 10 9 7
    ♡ K 8 6 5
    ♢ K 9 7
    ♣ A K

    Response: _____

5) ♠ J 9 8
    ♡ A Q
    ♢ K J 8 7
    ♣ A Q 7 6

    Response: _____

6) ♠ K J 10 9 7
    ♡ K 2
    ♢ K Q 9
    ♣ A 10 3

    Response: _____

EXERCISE THREE: OPENING AT THE TWO-LEVEL OR HIGHER

What is your opening bid with each of the following hands?

1)   ♠ K 10
      ♡ A Q 9 7
      ♢ K Q J 8
      ♣ A K J

Bid: _____

2)   ♠ A K J 10 9 8 7
      ♡ A K 4
      ♢ -
      ♣ A 9 4

Bid: _____

3)   ♠ A Q
      ♡ K Q 6
      ♢ A Q J 9 8
      ♣ A Q J

Bid: _____

4)   ♠ A J 10
      ♡ A K Q 9 8 7
      ♢ K J
      ♣ 8 5

Bid: _____

5)   ♠ A
      ♡ A 3
      ♢ A Q J 8 3
      ♣ A K J 10 6

Bid: _____

6)   ♠ 8 3
      ♡ 10
      ♢ 9 7 6
      ♣ A Q J 10 8 7 5

Bid: _____

EXERCISE FOUR: RESPONDING TO A TWO NO TRUMP OPENING BID

Your partner opens the bidding Two No Trump. What do you respond on each of the following hands?

1)   ♠ J 8 5 4
      ♡ 9 7 4
      ♢ 10 8 6 4
      ♣ 7 2

Response: _____

2)   ♠ 8 4
      ♡ J 9
      ♢ K J 9 7 4
      ♣ Q 8 4 2

Response: _____

3)   ♠ 9 7 6 5 3 2
      ♡ A 7
      ♢ J 8 6 4
      ♣ 3

Response: _____

4)   ♠ A 7 6
      ♡ K 10 8 5 3
      ♢ 9 6
      ♣ 8 3 2

Response: _____

5)   ♠ K J 10 7
      ♡ Q 9 7 6
      ♢ 5 4 3 2
      ♣ 4

Response: _____

6)   ♠ K 9 7
      ♡ Q J 3
      ♢ K 8 7 2
      ♣ Q 10 4

Response: _____

EXERCISE FIVE: RESPONDING TO A STRONG TWO-BID

Your partner opens the bidding Two Spades. What do you bid on the following hands?

1)   ♠ 9 8 4
      ♡ 10 7 6 4 2
      ♢ 8 5 3
      ♣ J 2

Response: _____

2)   ♠ K 8 6 4
      ♡ 5 4
      ♢ A J 8 7 6
      ♣ 6 3

Response: _____

3)   ♠ 8 6
      ♡ Q J 9 7 6 5
      ♢ 7
      ♣ 10 8 4 2

Response: _____

4)   ♠ A 8
      ♡ 6 4
      ♢ K Q 9 8 5 3
      ♣ 8 6 4

Response: _____

5)   ♠ 10 9 8 7
      ♡ Q 9 8 7 6
      ♢ -
      ♣ J 10 8 7

Response: _____

6)   ♠ 3
      ♡ K 10 8 7 5
      ♢ 8 4
      ♣ A Q 9 8 5

Response: _____

UNIT TWENTY-FOUR: PLAY OF THE CARDS

Joy of Bridge reference: pages 258 - 269

Declarer's objective during the play is to make his contract by taking at least the number of tricks for which his side has contracted. The defenders' objective is to take enough tricks to prevent declarer from making his contract.

EXERCISE ONE: COUNTING SURE TRICKS

How many sure tricks do you and your partner have in the following suit combinations?

DUMMY:	1) K 8 3	2) A Q 4	3) A J	4) A K 8	5) A K Q 4 3
DECLARER:	A 6 2	K 7 4	K Q	Q J	J 7 6
	___	___	___	___	___

EXERCISE TWO: PROMOTING CARDS

What is the maximum number of tricks you could take with each of the following suit combinations?

DUMMY:	1) 9 5 3	2) Q 10 3	3) Q 5	4) J 9 6 3	5) Q 8 3
DECLARER:	K Q J	J 6 5	K J 10 9	10 8 7 2	J 10 9 6 3
	___	___	___	___	___

EXERCISE THREE: ESTABLISHING LONG SUITS

What is the maximum number of tricks you could take with each of the following suit combinations?

DUMMY:	1) A 7 6 3	2) 9 8 7 6	3) A 8 3	4) K 6 4	5) A 9 6 4 2
DECLARER:	K 9 5 2	5 4 3 2	K 9 6 2	A Q 8 5 3	7 5 3
	___	___	___	___	___

EXERCISE FOUR: TRAPPING OPPONENTS' HIGH CARDS

What is the maximum number of tricks you could take with each of the following suit combinations?

DUMMY:	1) K 7	2) 8 5 3	3) A Q	4) Q J 10	5) Q 5 3
DECLARER:	5 2	K Q 6	9 5	A 6 4	A 6 4
	___	___	___	___	___

EXERCISE FIVE: TRUMPING LOSERS

Assume that Hearts are the trump suit and that the opponents lead the Ace of Spades, winning the first trick, and then the King of Spades. How many trump tricks will you win in each of the following situations?

DUMMY:	1) ♠ 7 5 ♡ 4 3 2	2) ♠ 7 ♡ 4 3 2	3) ♠ 7 5 ♡ 4 3 2
DECLARER:	♠ 8 4 ♡ A K Q J 10	♠ 8 4 ♡ A K Q J 10	♠ 8 ♡ A K Q J 10
	___	___	___

What is the advantage of trumping losers with dummy's trumps? Why is it not usually as advantageous to trump losers in the long hand (declarer's hand)?

_____ _____

LET'S EXPERIMENT

Construct the following hand, and place it face-up on the table:

Hand #35

```
                      ♠ 6 2
                      ♡ K 8 7
                      ♦ K Q J 10 9
                      ♣ 4 3 2

        ♠ Q J 10 9 4          N          ♠ 8 7 5
        ♡ 9 2                             ♡ 10 6 5 4 3
        ♦ A 8 4        W          E       ♦ 3 2
        ♣ 7 6 5                           ♣ A K J
                               S
                      ♠ A K 3
                      ♡ A Q J
                      ♦ 7 6 5
                      ♣ Q 10 9 8
```

Assume that South is the dealer. What would be the opening bid?

_____

Assuming that West says Pass, what would North respond?

_____

Assuming that East says Pass, what would South do? What would be the final contract?

_____   _____

What would be the opening lead?

_____

How many sure tricks does declarer have in Spades? In Hearts? In Diamonds? In Clubs?

_____   _____   _____   _____

Which suit offers the best opportunity to establish the additional tricks required by declarer to make his contract? How many additional tricks can be established?

_____   _____

Have each player pick up his hand. Start the bidding with South and complete the auction. Then play out the hand.

Did declarer take enough tricks to make the contract? Why should declarer establish the additional tricks he needs before taking his sure tricks in other suits?

_____   _____

Now construct the following hand, and place it face-up on the table:

Hand #36

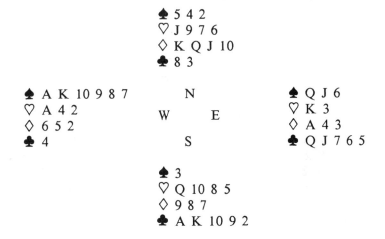

```
                          ♠ 5 4 2
                          ♡ J 9 7 6
                          ◇ K Q J 10
                          ♣ 8 3

        ♠ A K 10 9 8 7         N           ♠ Q J 6
        ♡ A 4 2          W         E        ♡ K 3
        ◇ 6 5 2                              ◇ A 4 3
        ♣ 4                    S            ♣ Q J 7 6 5

                          ♠ 3
                          ♡ Q 10 8 5
                          ◇ 9 8 7
                          ♣ A K 10 9 2
```

Assume that West is the dealer. What would be the opening bid?

_____

Assuming that North says Pass, what would East respond?

_____

Assuming that South says Pass, what would West rebid?

_____

Assuming that North says Pass, what would East rebid?

_____

Assuming that South, West and North all say Pass, what would be the final contract?

_____

Who will make the opening lead? What card will be led?

_____   _____

How many sure tricks does declarer have in Spades? In Hearts? In Diamonds? In Clubs?

_____   _____   _____   _____

Which suit offers the best opportunity to establish the additional trick required by declarer to make his contract? How can declarer establish the additional trick?

_____   _____

Have each player pick up his hand. Start the bidding with West and complete the auction. Then play out the hand.

Did declarer take enough tricks to make the contract? Why can declarer not afford to play all his Spade tricks before establishing his extra trick?

_____   _____

SUMMARY

TAKING TRICKS

There are two types of tricks.

1. _____ tricks which you can take without giving up the lead to the opponents.

2. _____ tricks which may be developed with a little work by:

   - *Promoting* cards

   - *Establishing* long suits

   - *Finessing* (trapping opponents' high cards)

   - *Trumping* losers

UNIT TWENTY-FIVE: PLANNING THE PLAY

Joy of Bridge reference: pages 270 - 282

Playing a bridge hand is like any other undertaking in that you must make a plan. Declarer's Four Questions will guide you in planning the play.

EXERCISE ONE: HOW MANY TRICKS DO I NEED?

How many tricks do you need to take in each of the following contracts?

Two Diamonds?   Four Spades?   Three No Trump?

_____   _____   _____

EXERCISE TWO: HOW MANY SURE TRICKS DO I HAVE?

How many sure tricks do you have in each suit in the following hand? In total?

DUMMY:
    ♠ K 8
    ♡ K 8 7
    ♢ K J 10 7
    ♣ 9 5 3 2

        N
   W   E
        S

DECLARER:
    ♠ A Q J 2
    ♡ A 6 5 2
    ♢ Q 9 5
    ♣ K 10

Spades	Hearts	Diamonds	Clubs	Total
_____	_____	_____	_____	_____

EXERCISE THREE: HOW CAN I BUILD EXTRA TRICKS?

Examine each combined suit in the hand from the previous exercise. How many extra tricks can you build in each suit? How?

Spades: ___   _____

Hearts: ___   _____

Diamonds: ___   _____

Clubs: ___   _____

EXERCISE FOUR: HOW DO I PUT IT ALL TOGETHER?

From your answers to the previous exercise, which suit offers the best opportunity to develop additional tricks? Why?

_____   _____

Assuming you are in a contract of Three No Trump and the opening lead is the Queen of Hearts, how would you play the hand in Exercise Two?

_____

LET'S EXPERIMENT

Construct the following hand, and place it face-up on the table:

Hand #37

```
                        ♠ 5 4
                        ♡ J 9 8 7
                        ◇ Q 10 8
                        ♣ A 5 3 2

   ♠ A Q J 10              N              ♠ 4 3 2
   ♡ K 3 2                                ♡ A 5 4 3
   ◇ K 5 4 2          W        E          ◇ A 7 6 3
   ♣ 8 7                                  ♣ K Q
                        S
                        ♠ K 8 7 6
                        ♡ Q 10
                        ◇ J 9
                        ♣ J 10 9 6 4
```

Assume that North is the dealer. Who would open the bidding? What would be the opening bid?

_____   _____

Assuming that South says Pass, what would West respond?

_____

Assuming that North says Pass, what would East rebid?

_____

Assuming South says Pass, what would West rebid? What would the final contract be?

_____   _____

Who will make the opening lead? What will the opening lead be?

_____   _____

How many tricks does declarer need to make his contract?

_____

How many sure tricks does declarer have?

_____

How can declarer build extra tricks in the Spade suit?

_____

How can declarer build extra tricks in the Heart suit?

_____

How can declarer build extra tricks in the Diamond suit?

_____

How can declarer build extra tricks in the Club suit?

_____

Which suit offers the best opportunity to establish the additional tricks required by declarer to make his contract?

_____

How does declarer put it all together?

_____

Have each player pick up his hand. Start the bidding with North and complete the auction. Then play out the hand.

Did declarer take enough tricks to make the contract? Why is it important that declarer not take his sure tricks in Hearts and Diamonds before building the extra Spade tricks?

_____   _____

Now construct the following hand, and place it face-up on the table:

Hand #38

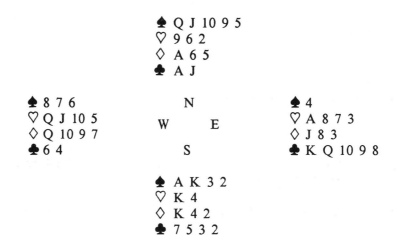

```
                          ♠ Q J 10 9 5
                          ♡ 9 6 2
                          ◇ A 6 5
                          ♣ A J

        ♠ 8 7 6             N            ♠ 4
        ♡ Q J 10 5                       ♡ A 8 7 3
        ◇ Q 10 9 7      W      E         ◇ J 8 3
        ♣ 6 4               S            ♣ K Q 10 9 8

                          ♠ A K 3 2
                          ♡ K 4
                          ◇ K 4 2
                          ♣ 7 5 3 2
```

Assume that East is the dealer. Who would open the bidding? What would be the opening bid?

———————   ———————

Assuming that West says Pass, what would North respond?

———————

Assuming that East says Pass, what would South rebid?

———————

Assuming that West says Pass, what would North rebid? What would be the final contract?

———————   ———————

Who will make the opening lead? What will the opening lead be?

———————   ———————

How many tricks does declarer need to make his contract?

———————

How many sure tricks does declarer have?

———————

Can declarer build extra tricks in the Spade suit?

———————

How can declarer build extra tricks in the Heart suit?

——

Can declarer build extra tricks in the Diamond suit?

_____

Can declarer build extra tricks in the Club suit?

_____

How does declarer put it all together?

_____

Have each player pick up his hand. Start the bidding with East and complete the auction. Then play out the hand.

Did declarer take enough tricks to make the contract? What two trick-building techniques can declarer use in the Heart suit?

_____   _____

SUMMARY

DECLARER'S FOUR QUESTIONS

1. _____

   - Add six to the level of your contract.

2. _____

   - Add together the number of sure tricks in each suit.

3. _____

   - By promoting high cards
   - By length
   - By leading toward high cards
   - By trumping losers (if playing in a trump contract)

4. _____

   - Choose from among your alternatives the safest and surest way of building the extra tricks needed to fulfill your contract.

UNIT TWENTY-SIX: THE DEFENDERS

Joy of Bridge reference: 283 - 295

During the play, the defenders' objective will be to try to take enough tricks to defeat the contract. Ideally, each defender should go through a series of questions to determine the best plan. They are basically the same as Declarer's Four Questions.

EXERCISE ONE: LEADS AGAINST NO TRUMP CONTRACTS

Which card should you lead from the following suits if you were defending against a No Trump contract?

1) K Q J 10   2) Q 9 7 6 3   3) Q J 10 7 4   4) A J 10 9   5) K 5 3

———   ———   ———   ———   ———

EXERCISE TWO: LEADS AGAINST SUIT CONTRACTS

Which card should you lead from the following suits if you were defending against a suit contract?

1) K Q 8 4   2) A K 6 5 2   3) Q 8 6   4) K 7 6 5 2   5) J 5

———   ———   ———   ———   ———

EXERCISE THREE: COVERING HONOURS

You are East. Which card should you play if declarer leads the indicated card from dummy (North)?

1) Dummy	2) Dummy	3) Dummy
7 6 **2**	**Q** 9 4	**Q** J 10
You	You	You
K 8 5 3	K 8 5 3	K 8 5 3

———   ———   ———

LET'S EXPERIMENT

Construct the following hand, and place it face-up on the table:

Hand #39

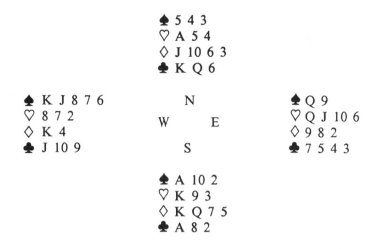

Assume that South is the dealer. What would be the opening bid?

————————

Assuming that West says Pass, what would North respond?

————————

Assuming that East says Pass, what would South do? What would be the final contract?

————————   ————————

What would be the opening lead? Why?

————————   ——————————————————————

Which card should East play to the first trick? Why?

————————   ——————————————————————

If East is allowed to win the first trick, which card should East lead next? Why?

————————   ——————————————————————

If West is allowed to win the second trick, which suit should he lead at trick three? Why?

————————   ——————————————————————

How many sure tricks does declarer have in Spades? In Hearts? In Diamonds? In Clubs?

————————   ————————   ————————   ————————

Which suit offers the best opportunity to establish the additional tricks required by declarer to make his contract? How does declarer plan to establish the additional tricks?

—————   ———————————————————————

Have each player pick up his hand. Start the bidding with South and complete the auction. Then play out the hand.

Did declarer take enough tricks to make the contract? If not, why not?

—————   ———————————————————————

On this hand, did it matter whether declarer won the first trick with the Ace of Spades or the second trick or the third? Can declarer make the contract against correct defense?

—————   —————

What would have happened if East had held the Ace of Diamonds instead of West?

———————————————————————

Now construct the following hand, and place it face-up on the table:

Hand #40

```
                    ♠ K J 9 3
                    ♡ 10 3 2
                    ◇ 10 7 6
                    ♣ J 10 9

    ♠ Q 7 6              N              ♠ 5 4 2
    ♡ Q 8 7                             ♡ A K J 4
    ◇ A Q 5 2        W       E          ◇ J 4 3
    ♣ K 4 2                             ♣ A 5 3
                        S
                    ♠ A 10 8
                    ♡ 9 6 5
                    ◇ K 9 8
                    ♣ Q 8 7 6
```

Assume that West is the dealer. What would be the opening bid?

—————

Assuming that North says Pass, what would East respond?

—————

Assuming that South says Pass, what would West rebid?

—————

Assuming that North says Pass, what would East rebid?

_____

Assuming that South, West and North all say Pass, what would be the final contract?

_____

Who would make the opening lead? What card would be led? Why?

_____   _____   _____

Which card would South play to the first trick? Which card would South play to the second trick? Why?

_____   _____   _____

Which card would North lead after the defense has taken the first four tricks?

_____

How many sure tricks does declarer have in Spades? In Hearts? In Diamonds? In Clubs?

_____   _____   _____   _____

Which suit offers the best opportunity to establish the additional trick required by declarer to make his contract?

_____

If declarer were to lead the Jack of Diamonds from dummy during the play, which card should South play? Why?

_____   _____

Have each player pick up his hand. Start the bidding with West and complete the auction. Then play out the hand.

Did declarer take enough tricks to make the contract? Can declarer make his contract against correct defense? If not, why not?

_____   _____   _____

What happens if the Jack of Diamonds is led and South does not cover with the King?

_____

If declarer takes his four sure tricks in Hearts before playing Diamonds, should the defenders discard Clubs or Diamonds? Without seeing declarer's hand, how might they know which suit to hold on to?

_____   _____

CHOOSING THE SUIT TO LEAD AGAINST A NO TRUMP CONTRACT

If partner has bid a suit, lead _____ suit.

Otherwise, lead your _____ suit.

With two equally long suits, lead the _____ suit.

CHOOSING THE SUIT TO LEAD AGAINST A TRUMP CONTRACT

If partner has bid a suit, lead _____ suit.

Otherwise:

- Lead a suit in which you have _____ high cards.

- Lead a _____ suit (other than the trump suit).

- Lead an _____ suit.

LEADING PARTNER'S SUIT

Lead the _____ of a doubleton (**A** 2, **K** 3).

Lead the _____ of touching high cards (**Q** J 7, K **J** 10).

Lead _____ from three or more cards when you lack touching high cards (Q 9 **3**, K J **5**, Q 7 6 **4**, 7 6 **3**).

LEADING YOUR SUIT

Lead the _____ of touching high cards (**K** Q J 3, **A** K 7 5 4 2).

Otherwise, lead _____ (K J 8 **4** 3, Q 9 7 **2**).

DEFENSIVE GUIDELINES

- Second player to a trick plays _____.

- Third player to a trick plays _____.

- _____ an honor with an honor.

APPENDIX I - BIDDING LADDER

		NOT VULNERABLE			VULNERABLE		
		Trick Score	Bonus	Total Score	Trick Score	Bonus	Total Score

SEVEN-LEVEL
(Grand Slam)

- 7 No Trump
- 7 Spades
- 7 Hearts
- 7 Diamonds
- 7 Clubs

SIX-LEVEL
(Small Slam)

- 6 No Trump
- 6 Spades
- 6 Hearts
- 6 Diamonds
- 6 Clubs

FIVE-LEVEL

- 5 No Trump
- 5 Spades
- 5 Hearts
- **5 Diamonds**
- **5 Clubs**

FOUR-LEVEL

- 4 No Trump
- **4 Spades**
- **4 Hearts**
- *4 Diamonds*
- *4 Clubs*

THREE-LEVEL

- **3 No Trump**
- *3 Spades*
- *3 Hearts*
- *3 Diamonds*
- *3 Clubs*

TWO-LEVEL

- *2 No Trump*
- *2 Spades*
- *2 Hearts*
- *2 Diamonds*
- *2 Clubs*

ONE-LEVEL

- *1 No Trump*
- *1 Spade*
- *1 Heart*
- *1 Diamond*
- *1 Club*

The Book
(6 Tricks)

Game contracts are in bold type.
Part-Game contracts are in italics.

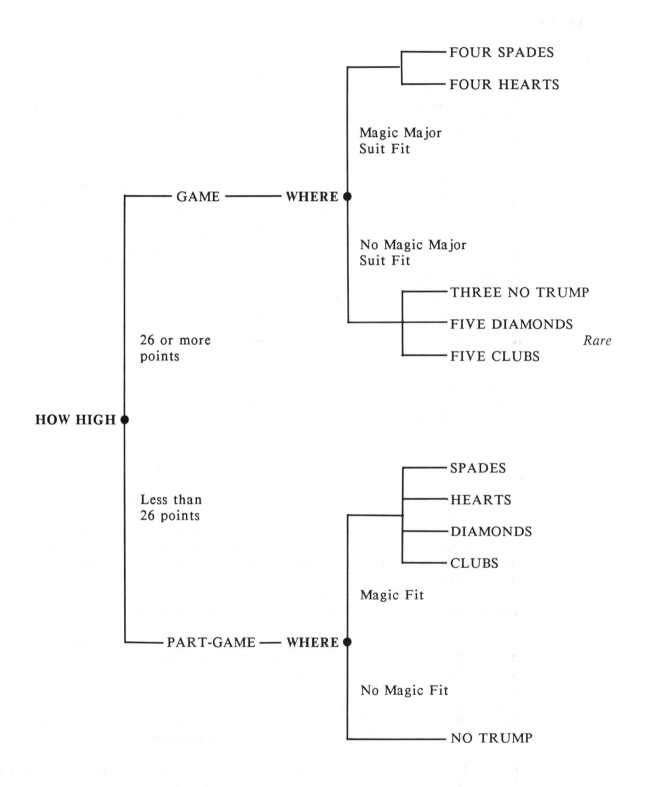

APPENDIX III - ANSWERS TO EXERCISES

UNIT ONE

EX. #1   Small cards sometimes take tricks because none of the other players have any cards left in the suit. This usually occurs when you have a long suit and two or three tricks have already been played.

High cards sometimes do not take tricks either because another player puts a higher card on the same trick or because you do not get an opportunity to lead the high card and end up having to discard it on a trick won by another player.

EX. #2   Predicting which cards you think will take tricks helps improve your memory. It is curiosity that helps you remember. You will probably find that you remembered more cards in your hand for this exercise than the previous one. Usually, a group of four players will predict taking more or less than the thirteen tricks available. This means there are surprises on every hand.

It is usually easiest to play last because you can see what everyone else has played before making your decision. If you play first, you get to choose the suit to play but may have difficulty deciding which card to lead. Playing in the middle of the trick is often difficult. You will often have to decide whether to play a high card or a low card. This becomes easier with practice. A few general guidelines are covered in the section on Play of the Hand in *The Joy of Bridge*.

EX. #3   Lead the King of Spades. You want to drive out the Ace and establish your remaining Spades as winning tricks. You want to keep your Aces in the other suits so that you can win later tricks and have the opportunity to take your Spade tricks. You should expect to take eight tricks.

EX. #4   1) Lead the Queen of Hearts. You should choose Hearts because it is your longest suit and represents the best chance of establishing additional tricks (by driving out the Ace and King). With touching high cards, you normally lead the top card.

2) Lead a low Spade (3 or 2). Your longest suit represents the best potential source of additional tricks. When you do not have touching high cards, you normally lead a low card (traditionally, the fourth best, the 3 in this case).

3) Lead the King of Hearts. This is similar to the first example. Opening leads are discussed in more detail in chapter 26 of the text.

EX. #5   It is both easier and more difficult to work with a partner. It is easier because there is someone across the table to help you take tricks. It is more difficult because you must work together but cannot see each other's hand.

If your partner leads a suit, it is often a good idea for you to help by leading the same suit when you have an opportunity to do so. This is an example of how you can work together with your partner.

EX. #6   When playing with a trump suit, short suits become important because you can "trump" (ruff) when you have no cards left in a suit.

EX. #7   You must often "negotiate" with your partner to try and get the longest combined suit named as the trump suit.

UNIT TWO

EX. #1   Seven; Eight; Nine.

EX. #2   One No Trump; One Club, Seven No Trump; Seven, Thirteen.

EX. #3   Important factors are your high cards (strength) and the length of your suits (distribution).

EX. #4   4-3-3-3, 4-4-3-2, 5-3-3-2 (suits could be in any order).

EX. #5   17 + 0 = 17; 13 + 1 = 14; 20 + 0 = 20; 13 + 2 = 15; 15 + 2 = 17; 18 + 0 = 18; Hands 1, 2 and 3 are balanced.

EX. #6   Hand 1; Hand 2 is balanced but not enough points, Hand 3 is balanced but too many points; Hand 5 is not balanced (contains a singleton).

EX. #7   One No Trump (balanced, 17 points); One Diamond (longest suit); One Club (lower-ranking of two 4-card suits); One Heart (longest suit); One Heart (higher-ranking of two 5-card suits); One Diamond (middle-ranking of three 4-card suits).

UNIT THREE

EX. #1   Game bonus levels are Three No Trump, Four Hearts, Four Spades, Five Clubs and Five Diamonds.

	NOT VULNERABLE			VULNERABLE		
	Trick Score	Bonus	Total Score	Trick Score	Bonus	Total Score
Three No Trump	100	300	400	100	500	600
Four Hearts	120	300	420	120	500	620
Four Spades	120	300	420	120	500	620
Five Clubs	100	300	400	100	500	600
Five Diamonds	100	300	400	100	500	600

EX. #2

	WE	THEY
i)		400
ii)	420	
iii)		110
iv)	650	

North-South won the round by 560 points (1070 - 510).

EX. #3

	WE	THEY
bonus for winning the rubber - 500		
overtrick from iv) - 30		
		40 - overtricks from iii)
i)		100
ii)	120	
iii)		20
iv)	120	

North-South won the rubber by 610 points (770 - 160).

UNIT FOUR

EX. #1   There are 40 High Card Points in the deck. If the partnership had all the high cards, they would take all the tricks. However, distribution could be used in place of High Card Points and, in practice, about 37 points are usually enough.
Three No Trump - 26; Four Hearts - 26; Four Spades - 26; Five Clubs - 29; Five Diamonds - 29.

EX. #2   Yes; Maybe; No.

EX. #3   Seven; Eight (Magic Fit).

EX. #4   No; Yes; Maybe; Six (partner has at least two); Two (partner has at most five). (Although, when you only have three cards, a Magic Fit is highly unlikely).

HAND #1   One No Trump; Three No Trump; Three No Trump; North, South, East; King of Hearts (longest suit, top of touching high cards); Nine.
Declarer should be able to take 9 tricks: 3 Spade tricks; 1 Heart trick; 5 Club tricks. With enough sure tricks to fulfill the contract, declarer should "take the tricks and run" (i.e. take his sure tricks).

HAND #2   One No Trump; Four Spades; Four Spades; West, East, North; Queen of Diamonds (longest suit, top of touching high cards); Ten.
Declarer should be able to take 10 tricks: 6 Spade tricks; 3 Heart tricks; 1 Club trick. With enough sure tricks in a suit contract, declarer should "draw trump" before taking his sure tricks in the other suits.

UNIT FIVE

EX. #1   1) 5 + 0 = 5; Part-Game; No Trump; Pass.
2) 1 + 2 = 3; Part-Game; Spades; Two Spades.
3) 5 + 1 = 6; Part-Game; Diamonds; Two Diamonds.
All three hands are in the range of 0 - 7 points. However, their distribution (shape) is different. The first hand is balanced; the other two are unbalanced.

EX. #2   1) 9 + 0 = 9; Maybe Game; No Trump; Two No Trump.
2) 7 + 1 = 8; Maybe Game; No Trump; Two No Trump.
3) 7 + 2 = 9; Maybe Game; No Trump; Two No Trump.

EX. #3   1) 11 + 1 = 12; Game; No Trump; Three No Trump.
2) 8 + 2 = 10; Game; Hearts; Four Hearts.
3) 8 + 2 = 10; Game; No Trump; Three No Trump.

EX. #4   1) 10 + 1 = 11; Game; Maybe Spades; Three Spades.
2) 11 + 1 = 12; Game; Maybe Hearts; Three Hearts.
In both cases you need to know whether partner has two, three or four cards in your Major suit.

HAND #3   One No Trump; Three No Trump; Pass, Three No Trump; South, North, West; King of Spades (longest suit, top of touching high cards); Nine.
Declarer should be able to take 9 tricks: 1 Spade trick; 3 Heart tricks; 1 Diamond trick; 4 Club tricks. When taking sure tricks in a suit, declarer should generally be careful to "take tricks in the short hand first."

HAND #4   One No Trump; Two Spades; Pass, East is captain, Two Spades; East, West, South; King of Clubs (top of touching high cards); Eight.
Declarer should be able to take 8 tricks: 4 Spade tricks; 2 Heart tricks; 2 Diamond tricks or, 3 Heart tricks and 1 Diamond trick if declarer takes the Queen, King and Ace of Hearts and discards a Diamond on the third Heart trick. Declarer can build additional tricks by "promoting" cards.

UNIT SIX

EX. #1   Two Hearts, Three No Trump, Four Spades, Two Diamonds.

EX. #2   Two No Trump, Opener can pass with a minimum (16 or 17 points) or bid Game with a maximum (18 points).

EX. #3   Three Hearts, Three Spades.

EX. #4   Three Hearts, Three Spades.

HAND #5   One No Trump; Three No Trump, Sign-off; Pass, Three No Trump; North, South, East; Queen of Spades; Nine.
Declarer should be able to take 9 tricks: 2 Spade tricks; 2 Heart tricks; 3 Diamond tricks; 2 Club tricks. Declarer can build an additional trick in his long suit by playing the Ace of Diamonds, then the King, then leading the suit again to establish a third trick.

HAND #6   One No Trump; Two No Trump, Invitational; Bids Three No Trump, Because he has a maximum (18 points), Three No Trump; East, West, South; Queen of Spades (longest suit, top of touching high cards); Nine.
Declarer should take nine tricks: 2 Spade tricks; 2 Heart tricks; 4 Diamond tricks; 1 Club trick. Declarer can build additional tricks by "trapping the opponents' high cards" (leading a Heart from dummy and "finessing" the Queen).

UNIT SEVEN

EX. #1   Four; Thirteen.
The hand is not very useful if partner opens One Heart; the Heart void is a disadvantage. The hand is much more valuable if partner opens One Spade; the Heart void will be useful if Spades are the trump suit.
Void - 5 points, Singleton - 3 points, Doubleton - 1 point.
You only use dummy points when you are planning to support partner's Major suit.
1) 10 + 5 = 15 dummy points; Four Spades.
2) 8 + 1 = 9 dummy points; Two Spades.
3) 9 + 3 = 12 dummy points; Three Spades.

EX. #2   Pass.

EX. #3   One Spade; One Spade (higher-ranking of two 5-card suits); One Heart (lower-ranking of two 4-card suits).

EX. #4   One No Trump; One No Trump; One No Trump.

EX. #5   Two Diamonds; Two Hearts (higher-ranking of two 5-card suits); Two Clubs (lower-ranking of two 4-card suits).

EX. #6   Two Diamonds; Three Diamonds; Three No Trump (Game).

EX. #7   Three Hearts; Pass; One Spade; One No Trump; Two Clubs; Two Hearts.

HAND #7   One Heart; Four Hearts; Four Hearts; Jack of Spades (top of touching high
          cards); Ten.
          Declarer should take ten tricks: 5 Heart tricks; 1 Diamond trick; 4 Club
          tricks. Declarer should play the Heart (trump) suit first (draw trump)
          when he has enough sure tricks to make his contract. When taking the Club
          tricks, declarer must be careful to play the Queen first, then go over to
          the Ace, King and Jack (take tricks in the short hand first).

HAND #8   One Spade; Two Spades; Two Spades; Queen of Hearts (top of touching high
          cards); Eight.
          Declarer should take eight tricks: 6 Spade tricks; 2 Diamond tricks. When
          playing in a trump suit, declarer can "trump losers in the dummy." By
          playing the Ace and King of Diamonds and then leading the Two and putting
          a Spade on it, declarer ends up with six Spade tricks rather than five.

UNIT EIGHT

EX. #1   Here are some example hands. Your hands may look different.

Minimum	Medium	Maximum
♠ A 3	♠ A K	♠ A K
♡ K J 7 5 2	♡ K J 7 5 2	♡ K J 7 5 2
◇ A 5 4 3	◇ A 5 4 3	◇ A K 4 3
♣ J 6	♣ J 6	♣ J 6

EX. #2   Minimum, Two Spades; Maximum, Four Spades; Medium, Three Spades.

EX. #3   Minimum, One Spade; Medium, One Heart (lower-ranking of two 4-card suits);
          Maximum, Two Spades (Jump Shift).

EX. #4   Minimum, One No Trump; Maximum, Two No Trump; Minimum, One Spade
          (Question Two before Question Three).

EX. #5   Minimum, Two Clubs; Medium, Two Clubs; Maximum, Three Clubs (Jump
          Shift); Minimum, Two Diamonds; Medium, Three Diamonds; Minimum, Two
          Diamonds. Don't bid a higher-ranking suit at the two-level with a minimum.

HAND #9   One Club; One Heart; Two Hearts; Two Hearts; Queen of Diamonds, Eight.
          Declarer should take eight tricks: 2 Spade tricks; 2 Heart tricks; 4 Club
          tricks. Declarer should draw trumps before trying to take his sure
          tricks. Sometimes, declarer will have to lose tricks to the opponents when
          drawing trumps. Don't be afraid to lose some tricks to the opponents, as
          long as you still make enough tricks for your contract.

HAND #10 One Diamond; One Spade; One No Trump; One No Trump; King of Hearts.
          Since you lead the top of touching high cards, the lead of the King tells
          partner that you have the next lower card, the Queen, but do not have the
          next higher card, the Ace.
          Declarer needs seven tricks. He should take seven tricks: 3 Spade tricks;
          1 Heart trick; 1 Diamond trick; 2 Club tricks. Declarer must drive out the
          opponent's Ace of Spades to establish the extra tricks needed. He should
          start by playing the Jack first (high card from the short hand).

UNIT NINE

EX. #1   Two Hearts; Two Diamonds; Four Hearts.

EX. #2   Three Hearts; Two No Trump; Two Spades; Four Hearts; Three No Trump; Three Diamonds.

HAND #11   One Spade; Two Hearts; Four Hearts; Four Hearts; Queen of Clubs. Declarer should take ten tricks: 2 Spade tricks; 5 Heart tricks; 3 Diamond tricks. After losing three Club tricks, declarer can avoid losing a trump trick by leading a Heart from the dummy and, if West plays low, "taking a finesse." Declarer could still make the contract if West had the K 7 3 of Hearts but would need to finesse twice. To provide for this possibility, declarer should lead the Ten (or Nine or Eight) from the dummy, planning to play a low card from his hand. If the finesse is successful, declarer will still be leading from the dummy and can repeat the finesse.

HAND #12   One Heart; Two Clubs; Two No Trump; Three No Trump, West; Low Spade. North should lead his longest suit. With no touching high cards, he should lead low (traditionally, the fourth best, the 5 in this case). Declarer should take nine tricks: 2 Spade tricks; 2 Heart tricks; 1 Diamond trick; 4 Club tricks. Declarer can get the extra tricks required to make the contract by "establishing a long suit," Clubs in this case. By playing the suit three times, losing one trick to the opponents, the remaining two Clubs in the dummy will be established as tricks. Declarer should win the first trick with the King of Spades. After establishing the extra Club tricks, declarer will need a way to get to the dummy to play the two Club tricks. The Ace of Spades can serve as the "entry" to dummy once the Club tricks have been established.

UNIT TEN

EX. #1   6 - 10 points, 11 - 12 points, 13 - 16 points; Invitational, Invitational, Invitational (opener would only continue bidding if interested in a Slam contract); Hearts, HOW HIGH.

EX. #2   1) One Heart, Minimum, Pass.
             2) One Heart, Medium, Three Hearts.
             3) One Heart, Maximum, Four Hearts.

EX. #3   1) One Spade, Minimum, Pass (with a "minimum" minimum).
             2) One Spade, Minimum, Four Spades (with a "maximum" minimum).
             3) One Spade, Medium, Four Spades.

EX. #4   1) One Heart, Minimum, Pass.
             2) One Heart, Medium, Five Hearts (Inviting Slam - see Unit 22).
             3) One Heart, Maximum, Six Hearts (Slam - see Unit 22).

HAND #13   No, East, One Heart; Two Hearts, Four Hearts, Four Hearts; South, Queen of Diamonds. The lead of Queen tells your partner that you also have the Jack but that you do not have the King.
Declarer has ten tricks: 2 Spade tricks; 4 Heart tricks (after driving out the opponents' Ace and King); 1 Diamond trick; 3 Club tricks. However, the opponents have led Diamonds, forcing out declarer's Ace. If declarer starts by drawing trump, the opponents will win the trick and be able to take two Diamond tricks immediately. This will give them four tricks in total, enough to defeat the contract.

Instead, declarer must take his three Club tricks first (playing the King first then the Four over to the Ace and Queen). On the third Club trick, declarer can discard one of his Diamonds. Now it is safe to draw trumps, since the opponents can only take one Diamond trick before declarer becomes void and is able to trump. Declarer will only lose two Heart tricks and one Diamond trick.

Declarer may delay drawing trumps if he needs to trump losers in the dummy or get rid of losers quickly by discarding them on other winning tricks.

HAND #14　No, South, One Diamond; Three Diamonds, Pass, Three Diamonds.
Declarer should take nine tricks: 3 Spade tricks; 4 Diamond tricks; 2 Club tricks. Declarer should play the Ace of Diamonds in case one of the opponents has a singleton King, and then lead toward the Queen trying to "trap" the King if West has it. Declarer should not lead the Queen from dummy. Even if East had the King, he could "cover" the Queen with the King, to make declarer play the Ace. Since the opponents have the Jack and the Ten, they might still end up with two tricks. Only lead a high card if you can afford to have it covered. Otherwise, lead toward your high card.

UNIT ELEVEN

EX. #1　　1) Part-Game, No Trump, Pass.
　　　　　2) Part-Game, Diamonds, Two Diamonds.
　　　　　3) Part-Game, Hearts, Two Hearts.

EX. #2　　1) Maybe Game, Hearts, Three Hearts.
　　　　　2) Maybe Game, No Trump, Two No Trump.
　　　　　3) Maybe Game, Spades, Three Spades.

EX. #3　　1) Game, No Trump, Three No Trump.
　　　　　2) Game, Hearts, Four Hearts.
　　　　　3) Game, Hearts or No Trump, Two Diamonds (new suit).

EX. #4　　The Bidding Analysis Chart will help guide you to an appropriate contract. With 26 or more points, you should be in a Game contract; with less than 26, you should be in Part-Game. If you are in a Game contract, with a Magic Major Suit Fit, you should be playing Game in the Major suit; otherwise, in Three No Trump. If you are in Part-Game, you should be playing in a suit if you have a Magic Fit; otherwise, in No Trump.

HAND #15　No, North, One Club; One Heart; One No Trump; Pass, One No Trump.
East should lead a low Spade (traditionally, the fourth best, the Three). East should lead his longest suit and, with no touching high cards, should lead low.
Declarer can count two tricks in the Spade suit after the opening lead. If West plays the King, declarer can win with the Ace and the Queen will now be the highest remaining card in the suit. If West does not play the King, declarer can win with the Queen and still have the Ace left.
Declarer should take seven tricks: 2 Spade tricks; 1 Heart trick; 2 Diamond tricks; 2 Club tricks. Declarer can give himself the best chance of winning two Diamond tricks by leading (twice) toward his King and Queen. Provided West has the Ace, declarer will win tricks with both the King and the Queen. Declarer will need to use the Ace of Hearts and the Ace of Clubs as "entries" to the dummy to lead toward the Diamonds.
It would make a difference if East had the Ace of Diamonds. Now declarer would only get one Diamond trick and be unable to make his contract.

HAND #16   No; One Diamond; One Heart; Two Hearts, Minimum (13 - 16 points); Three Hearts, Invitational (11 - 12 points); Four Hearts, upper range (15 - 16 points); Ten of Spades, telling partner he has the Nine but not the Jack. Declarer should take ten tricks: 1 Spade trick (after the opponents take their Ace and Queen; 4 Heart tricks; 4 Diamond tricks; 1 Club trick. To avoid losing a trick to the opponent's Queen of Hearts, declarer must trap it by leading a Heart from dummy and "taking a finesse."

UNIT TWELVE

EX. #1   1) Part-Game, Hearts, Pass.
             2) Game, Hearts, Four Hearts.
             3) Game, Hearts, Four Hearts.

EX. #2   1) Game, No Trump, Three No Trump.
             2) Game, Hearts (since opener bid Hearts before Clubs he must have five of them), Four Hearts.
             3) Game, Spades or No Trump, Three Diamonds (new suit).

HAND #17   Pass, West, One Heart; One Spade; Three Spades; Pass, Three Spades. Declarer should take nine tricks: 6 Spade tricks; 2 Heart tricks; 1 Club trick. Declarer can avoid losing two Club tricks by trumping the losing Clubs in dummy. Declarer could also discard one on dummy's fourth Diamond if it becomes established as a trick and trumps have been drawn. Declarer might take a Heart finesse by leading toward the Jack and later discarding a Club on one of the high Hearts but this would be a risky line of play.

HAND #18   South, One Diamond (too strong for One No Trump); One Heart; Two No Trump; Three No Trump, South's bid is forcing - showing a maximum hand - Three No Trump.
West should lead his longest suit, Spades, and, with no touching high cards, should lead low, the Five. East should win the first trick with the Ace and lead back the Jack. He should lead back a Spade because it is the suit his partner led. He leads the Jack because it is the top of his (remaining) doubleton.
Declarer should take nine tricks: 1 Spade trick (after the opponents' have taken the Ace); 2 Heart tricks; 4 Diamond tricks; 2 Club tricks. Declarer establishes the additional Diamond tricks through length. After playing the suit three times, the opponents will have no Diamonds left and declarer's remaining Diamonds will be established as tricks.

REVIEW QUESTIONS FOR BIDDING WITHOUT COMPETITION

EX. #1   One Heart (longest suit); One No Trump; One Heart (higher-ranking of two 5-card suits); One Diamond (lower-ranking of two 4-card suits); One Heart (middle-ranking of three 4-card suits); Pass (less than 13 points).

EX. #2   Three No Trump; Two Spades; Two No Trump; Four Hearts; Pass; Three Spades.

EX. #3   One Spade; Three Hearts; One No Trump; Pass; Two Diamonds; Two Hearts.

EX. #4   One Spade; One Heart; One No Trump; Two Diamonds; Three No Trump; Three Diamonds.

EX. #5   One Spade; One No Trump; Two Hearts; Three Clubs; Two Diamonds; Two No Trump.

EX. #6   Three Hearts; Four Hearts; Two No Trump; Three No Trump; Three Clubs; Two Spades.

EX. #7   Pass; Three No Trump; Two Spades; Two No Trump; Two Diamonds; Three Spades.

EX. #8   Two Hearts; Two Spades; Pass; Two No Trump; Three Hearts; Three No Trump.

UNIT THIRTEEN

EX. #1   50 + 50 = 100; 100 + 200 = 300; 100 + 100 = 200; 200 + 300 = 500.

EX. #2   60 + 50 = 110; 120 + 300 + 50 = 470; 60 + 50 = 110; 120 + 500 + 50 = 670.

EX. #3   120 + 300 = 420; 240 + 300 + 50 = 590; 120 + 500 = 620; 240 + 500 + 50 = 790.

UNIT FOURTEEN

EX. #1   You might be able to make a Part-Game or Game contract. You might make it more difficult for the opponents to exchange information. You may push the opponents to a higher contract than they can make. You may provide your partner with enough information to help him defeat the opponents' contract.

EX. #2   You might be doubled or left to go down undoubled. You might give the opponents useful information.

EX. #3   One Spade; One No Trump; Pass.

UNIT FIFTEEN

EX. #1   1) 3 + 0 = 3 dummy points; Pass.
              2) 7 + 1 = 8 dummy points; Two Hearts.
              3) 9 + 3 = 12 dummy points; Three Hearts.

EX. #2   Here is a sample hand. Your hand may look different.

♠ J 9 6 5 3
♥ 7 6
♦ Q 8 2
♣ 9 5 4

EX. #3   One Spade; Pass; Two Hearts (raise partner with 3-card support).

EX. #4   One No Trump; Two Diamonds; Three No Trump (Game).

HAND #19   South, One Diamond; Overcall One Heart; Two Hearts; Four Hearts; Four Hearts. North should lead a Diamond because his partner has bid that suit. With a doubleton, lead the top card, the Five. After winning the first Diamond trick, South should lead his other high Diamond and then lead the suit again so that his partner can trump it. South knows that North has no more Diamonds because North led the Five and then played the Two, showing a doubleton. If North had started with three or more Diamonds, he would have led a low one first.

Declarer should take ten tricks: 3 Spade tricks; 6 Heart tricks; 1 Club trick. Declarer can avoid losing a Club trick by discarding his Seven of Clubs on dummy's Ace of Spades, after taking tricks with the King and Queen of Spades. Declarer will have to be careful. The only entry to dummy is the King of Hearts. Declarer must take tricks with the King and Queen of Spades before taking a trick with the King of Hearts.

HAND #20   West, One Spade; Overcall One No Trump; Two No Trump; Pass (minimum hand), Two No Trump.
East should lead a Spade because his partner bid the suit. With three cards and no touching high cards, West should lead low, the Two. Some players prefer to lead the top or middle card from three small cards but this is more likely to make it difficult for your partner to know how many cards you started with.
Declarer should take eight tricks: 2 Spade tricks; 2 Heart tricks; 2 Diamond tricks; 2 Club tricks. Declarer must establish the extra Club tricks by leading the suit as soon as he wins the first Spade trick and leading it again when he next wins a trick. Declarer can actually establish three extra tricks in Clubs by driving out the Ace and King. However, the opponents will have established their Spade suit in the meantime (by driving out declarer's Ace and King) and declarer will have to discard one of the established Clubs on one of the defenders' Spade tricks.

UNIT SIXTEEN

EX. #1   Pass; Three Hearts; Four Hearts.

EX. #2   Pass; Pass; Pass.
Pass; One Heart; One No Trump.
If partner overcalls at the two-level, responder has to Pass with a minimum hand (6 - 10 points) as well as a weak hand (0 - 5 points).

EX. #3   Three Diamonds; Three No Trump; Two Spades.

HAND #21   One Spade; Overcall Two Hearts; Four Hearts; Pass, Four Hearts.
South should lead his singleton Spade, the Eight, because his partner bid the suit. After winning the first Spade trick, North should continue to take his other two Spade tricks. He knows that declarer cannot trump the third Spade trick because his partner had only a singleton.
North might then lead another Spade. He does not expect to win the trick because he knows that East has no more Spades and will be able to trump. However, South also has no Spades left and may be able to put on a higher trump and win the trick for the defense. To prevent this happening, East must be careful to trump with the Ten (or higher), not with the Two.
Declarer should take ten tricks: 5 Heart tricks; 2 Diamond tricks; 3 Club tricks. Declarer avoids losing a Club trick by playing a Club to dummy's King and then leading a Club back toward the Ace and Jack, finessing the Jack if North does not play the Queen. Declarer could make the contract if South held the Queen of Clubs by playing the Ace first and then leading the Jack, finessing if South does not cover. On this hand, it is most likely that North holds the Queen of Clubs because North opened the bidding.

HAND #22   One Heart; Overcall Two Diamonds; Three Diamonds; Three No Trump (Game).
West should lead the Nine of Hearts, top of a doubleton in the suit that his partner bid. This will help partner establish his Heart suit by driving out declarer's Ace.

Declarer should take ten tricks: 2 Spade tricks; 1 Heart trick; 5 Diamond tricks (after driving out West's King); 2 Club tricks. However, if South wins the first trick with the Ace of Hearts and then drives out West's King of Diamonds, West will have the Two of Hearts left to lead over to partner. East will now be able to take four Heart tricks and defeat the contract. To prevent this, South should not take the Ace of Hearts at the first trick. He should "hold up" his Ace and use it to win the second or third trick. The advantage of this play is that, when West wins a trick with the King of Diamonds, he will have no Hearts left to lead to East and will be unable to defeat the contract.

UNIT SEVENTEEN

EX. #1   Double; Pass; Double.

EX. #2   Two Hearts; Pass; Double; One No Trump; Double; Pass.

UNIT EIGHTEEN

EX. #1   One Heart; One Spade (longer suit); Two Clubs.
These hands are all weak (0 - 5 points) or minimum (6 - 10 points).

EX. #2   Two Hearts; Three Clubs; Two No Trump.
These hands are in the 11 - 12 point range. Responder wants to invite Game.

EX. #3   Four Spades; Three No Trump; Four Hearts.
These hands have 13 or more points. Responder wants to be in Game.

HAND #23   North, One Heart; Double; Two Diamonds; Pass, Two Diamonds.
Declarer should take nine tricks: 2 Spade tricks; 5 Diamond tricks (by ruffing a losing Heart in the dummy); 2 Club tricks. Declarer can avoid losing two Club tricks by leading the Jack and, if North plays low, playing low from dummy. South will win this trick with the Queen. However, later West can repeat the finesse by leading the Ten and, if North plays low, playing low from dummy again. The Ten will win the trick because South does not have both the King and the Queen.

HAND #24   One Club; Pass, Double; One Spade; Two Spades; Four Spades (South is showing a medium hand of 17 - 18 points), Four Spades.
Declarer should take at least ten tricks (possibly twelve): 6 Spade tricks (by ruffing a losing Club with one of dummy's trumps); 3 or 4 Heart tricks; 1 Diamond trick; 1 Club trick (by leading toward the King if the opponents have not already taken their Ace). Declarer can avoid losing a trump trick by leading the Queen from dummy and, if West plays low, finessing by playing a low card from his hand. In a similar fashion, declarer can lead the Jack of Hearts from his hand and, if East does not play the Queen, play low from dummy and win the trick. If declarer finesses twice (by next leading the Ten of Hearts), he can actually take four Heart tricks.

UNIT NINETEEN

EX. #1   One Spade; One Spade; One No Trump.

EX. #2   Four Spades; Two No Trump; Two Spades (3-card support in competition).

EX. #3   Two Hearts; One Spade; One No Trump.

EX. #4   Two Spades; Three Spades; Pass.

EX. #5   Pass; Two Spades; Three Spades.

HAND #25 South, One Spade; Double, Two Spades, Three Hearts; Four Hearts; Pass, Four Hearts. After winning the first two Spade tricks, South should lead another suit: either the Ten of Diamonds (top of touching high cards) or the Five of Clubs (low from three or more cards with no touching high cards). South should not lead another Spade because neither dummy nor declarer have any. Leading another Spade would allow declarer to trump (ruff) in dummy and discard (sluff) a losing Club from his hand. Giving declarer a "ruff and sluff" is usually not a good play for the defense. Declarer should take ten tricks: 6 Heart tricks; 2 Diamond tricks; 2 Club tricks. Declarer can get two Club tricks by leading a Club from has hand toward dummy and, if South plays low, playing the Nine (or Ten or Jack) from the dummy. North can win the Queen but later declarer can repeat the finesse, leading low from his hand and playing the Ten (or Jack) when South follows low. Playing the Club suit in this fashion, declarer will only lose two Club tricks if North has both the King and the Queen, which is very unlikely. Declarer should also play the Nine (or Ten or Jack) from the dummy if South led a low Club at trick three.

HAND #26 South, One Diamond; One Spade, Two Clubs, Pass; Two No Trump, Pass, Three No Trump; Three No Trump.
West should lead a low Spade, the Seven. He is trying to defeat the contract by establishing enough tricks in his longest suit. Without touching high cards, he leads low (traditionally, fourth best).
Declarer should take at least nine tricks: 1 Spade trick; 3 Heart tricks; 1 Diamond trick; 4 Club tricks. If East plays the Queen of Spades at trick one, declarer should win the Ace. Playing the Ten under the Queen would waste the value of that card when dummy has the Nine. In this case, if declarer holds up with the Ace, the opponents may defeat the contract, ending up with four Spade tricks and the Ace of Clubs. Try it and see. You might want to contrast this hand with #22.

REVIEW QUESTIONS FOR BIDDING WITH COMPETITION

EX. #1   One Spade; One No Trump; Pass; Two Clubs; Two Diamonds; Pass.

EX. #2   Pass; Two Hearts; One Spade; One No Trump; Two Diamonds; Four Hearts.

EX. #3   Double; Pass; Two Hearts; Double; One No Trump; Double.

EX. #4   Two Clubs; One Spade; Two Spades; Four Spades; Three No Trump; Three Diamonds.

EX. #5   Pass; Two Spades; Four Hearts; Three Spades; Two No Trump; Three No Trump.

UNIT TWENTY

EX. #1   Yes, Four Spades; No, Three No Trump; Maybe, Two Clubs; Maybe, Two Clubs; Maybe, Three Hearts; Maybe, Two Clubs.

EX. #2   Two Hearts; Two Spades; Two Diamonds.

EX. #3   Four Hearts; Three No Trump; Four Hearts.

EX. #4   Three Spades; Two No Trump; Three Hearts.

HAND #27   West, One No Trump; Two Clubs, Two Hearts, Four Hearts, Four Hearts.
            Declarer should take ten tricks: 1 Spade trick, 4 Heart tricks, 2 Diamond
            tricks, 3 Club tricks. In a contract of Three No Trump, North would lead a
            Spade and West's Ace would be driven out. When West tried to establish the
            extra tricks needed to make the contract by driving out the Ace of Clubs,
            North and South could win the Ace and take four Spade tricks, defeating the
            contract.

HAND #28   North, One No Trump; Two Clubs, Two Diamonds, Two No Trump, Three
            No Trump (North has a maximum); Three No Trump, Queen of Spades.
            Declarer should take nine tricks: 2 Spade tricks; 1 Heart trick; 4 Diamond
            tricks; 2 Club tricks. Declarer must establish the extra tricks needed
            using the Diamond suit.
            If he plays the Ace and King first, then give the opponents a Diamond
            trick, he will have established dummy's remaining two Diamonds as good
            tricks but will not have an entry to the dummy allowing him to reach them.
            To overcome this, declarer should give up a Diamond trick to the opponents
            first, by playing little Diamonds from both hands, before taking the Ace
            and King. When declarer regains the lead, he can now take the Ace and King
            of Diamonds and end up in the dummy to take the other two Diamond tricks.

UNIT TWENTY-ONE

EX. #1   Two No Trump; Two Spades; Two Diamonds.

EX. #2   Three No Trump; Four Hearts; Three Clubs (Stayman Convention).

EX. #3   Three Spades; Two No Trump; Three Clubs.

HAND #29   East, Two Spades. West would respond Two No Trump because he cannot Pass
            opener's Two Spade bid but wants to show a weak hand (0 - 5 points).
            East would rebid Three Hearts to show his second suit. His partner already
            knows about his Spades and can infer that he has at least five of them
            since he bid Spades first. This is more informative than rebidding Three
            Spades.
            West would rebid Four Hearts. He still cannot Pass because the partnership
            is forced to Game by East's opening bid.
            East would now Pass. He has shown his strong hand and West, the Captain,
            has determined where the contract should be played.
            Declarer should take eleven tricks: 4 Spade tricks; 5 Heart tricks; 1
            Diamond trick; 1 Club trick. Declarer can avoid losing a trump trick by
            taking a finesse. Declarer can get to dummy by leading the Ace of Spades
            and then leading one of his little Spades and trumping it with one of
            dummy's Hearts. Declarer should now lead the Jack (or Ten or Nine) of
            Hearts from the dummy and, if North does not cover with the King, play low
            from his hand. Now declarer is still in dummy and can repeat the finesse.
            Declarer should not take the Ace and the King and the Queen of Spades
            before trying to trump a little one in dummy. If he does this, North will
            also have no Spades left and will be able to "overtrump" the trump played
            from dummy. Declarer only needs to trump one of his little Spades in dummy
            because later, after drawing the opponents' trumps, he can play his
            remaining high Spades and the opponents will have no Spades left.
            Declarer's remaining little Spade will be an established trick.

HAND #30   South, Two No Trump; Pass, Four Spades, Pass; Pass, Responder is Captain
            and made a sign-off bid; Four Spades; Queen Of Hearts, top of touching high
            cards.
            Declarer should take ten tricks: 6 Spade tricks; 1 Diamond trick; 3 Club
            tricks. Declarer can avoid losing a Diamond trick if he can throw his
            Diamond away on an established Club trick in the dummy. To establish the
            Club suit, declarer must take the Ace and the King and then lead another
            Club and trump it. Now the opponents have no more Clubs and the remaining
            Clubs in dummy are established as tricks. Declarer can use one of the
            established Clubs to discard his losing Diamond. Declarer could still make
            the contract if the opponents' Clubs were divided four-two. He would have
            to play the Ace and King and trump a Club. He would then have to go back
            to dummy and lead another Club and trump it. Now the opponents would
            have no Clubs left and dummy's remaining Club would be an established
            trick. Note that declarer would have to be very careful with his entries
            to the dummy. He would have to delay drawing trumps and use one of
            dummy's high trumps as an entry to lead the fourth round of Clubs and
            another high trump to get to dummy and take the established Club trick.

UNIT TWENTY-TWO

EX. #1   Slam; Game; Maybe Slam.

EX. #2   Six Hearts; Five Hearts; Seven Hearts; Four Hearts; One Spade; Six Hearts.

EX. #3   Pass; Pass; Six No Trump.

EX. #4   Six Spades; Five Spades; Pass.

HAND #31   One Spade; Four Spades, Six Spades, Six Spades.
            Declarer should take twelve tricks: 6 Spade tricks; 3 Heart tricks; 1
            Diamond trick; 2 Club tricks. If West has led the King of Diamonds and
            driven out South's Ace, there is the danger that the defenders will be able
            to take a Diamond trick when declarer trys to establish the Club suit.
            Since there is no way to avoid losing a trick to the Ace of Clubs, declarer
            must try to avoid losing a Diamond trick as well. After drawing trumps,
            declarer should play the Ace, King and Queen of Hearts, discarding two
            Diamonds from dummy. Now dummy has no Diamonds left and it is safe for
            declarer to drive out the opponents' Ace of Clubs to establish the
            additional tricks needed to make the contract.

HAND #32   Two No Trump; Four No Trump, Six No Trump, Six No Trump.
            Declarer should take twelve tricks: 3 Spade tricks; 3 Heart tricks; 3
            Diamond tricks; 3 Club tricks. Declarer can establish the three tricks in
            Clubs by driving out the opponents' Ace. He must do this before taking
            his sure tricks in the other suits.

UNIT TWENTY-THREE

EX. #1   Three Clubs; One Spade; Four Hearts.

EX. #2   Pass; Three Hearts; Three No Trump.

EX. #3   Four Hearts; Three No Trump; Four Hearts.

EX. #4   Pass; Three Hearts; Double.

HAND #33 Three Diamonds; Pass, Pass, Pass, Three Diamonds.
Declarer should take eight tricks: 1 Heart trick; 6 Diamond tricks; 1 Club trick. The defense might slip and allow declarer to make a second Club trick and make his contract. It is not a poor result for North and South if the contract is defeated. East and West can make at least a Part-Game in Spades.
If North passed, East would open the bidding One Spade and West would raise to Three Spades. East would probably Pass because he has a "minimum" minimum and East West would play the contract in Part-Game. West will be able to take at least nine tricks (probably ten with the fortunate location of the King of Spades).

HAND #34 South, Three Hearts; Double, Pass, Three Spades; Pass, Four Spades? West will probably carry on to Game, hoping that East has six or more points. The final contract will be Three or, more likely, Four Spades. East and West have been pushed into a poor contract so the pre-emptive opening bid was a success.
Declarer will be hard-pressed to take more than eight tricks: 4 Spade tricks (if he is careful!); 1 Heart trick; 2 Diamond tricks; 1 Club trick (maybe!). East and West should not be discouraged by the result. Their actions were reasonable. Instead, South should be congratulated on his pre-emptive opening bid, which made the auction very difficult for his opponents.
If South had passed originally, West would open One Diamond and may have been left to play there. This would be a reasonable contract and West would probably make it.
East should not have passed his partner's take-out Double. This would have led to a worse result since, with careful play, South will probably make his contract of Three Hearts.

REVIEW QUESTIONS FOR MORE ON BIDDING

EX. #1   Two Clubs (Stayman Convention); Three Spades; Two Clubs (intending to show an invitational hand with five or more Hearts); Pass; Two Clubs; Two Clubs.

EX. #2   Two Spades; Two Hearts; Two Diamonds; Two Hearts; Two Diamonds; Two Spades.

EX. #3   Two No Trump; Two Spades; Three No Trump; One Heart; Two Diamonds; Three Clubs.

EX. #4   Pass; Three No Trump; Four Spades; Three Hearts; Three Clubs (Stayman Convention); Six No Trump.

EX. #5   Two No Trump; Three Spades; Two No Trump; Three Diamonds; Three Spades; Three Hearts.

UNIT TWENTY-FOUR

EX. #1   Two; Three; Two; Three; Four (but likely five unless one opponent has all five of the missing cards).

EX. #2   Two; One; Three; One; Three.

EX. #3   Three; One; Three; Five; Three.

EX. #4   One; Two; Two; Three; Two.

EX. #5   Five; Six; Five.
          Trumping losers with dummy's trumps usually gains a trick for declarer.
          Trumping losers in declarer's hand does not usually gain a trick.

HAND #35 One No Trump; Three No Trump; Pass, Three No Trump; Queen of Spades;
          Two, Three, None, None; Diamonds, Four.
          Declarer should take nine tricks: 2 Spade tricks; 3 Heart tricks; 4 Diamond
          tricks. Declarer should not take his sure tricks in Hearts and Spades
          before establishing his extra tricks in Diamonds because that will only
          establish tricks for his opponents.

HAND #36 One Spade; Two Clubs; Two Spades; Four Spades; Four Spades; North, King
          of Diamonds; Six, Two, One, None.
          Declarer can use the Heart suit to establish an extra trick. He can do
          that by trumping his losing Heart with one of dummy's Spades.
          Declarer should take ten tricks: 7 Spade tricks (including the trick
          gained by trumping the losing Heart); 2 Heart tricks; 1 Diamond trick.
          Declarer cannot afford to play all his Spade tricks first, because he needs
          to have a Spade left in dummy with which to trump his losing Heart.

UNIT TWENTY-FIVE

EX. #1   Eight; Ten; Nine.

EX. #2   Four; Two; None; None; Six.

EX. #3   Spades: None - you cannot take more than your four sure tricks.
          Hearts: One - you could try playing the suit three times. If each opponent
          started with three Hearts, your last remaining Heart would be established
          as a sure trick.
          Diamonds: Three - you can promote your Diamonds into tricks by driving out
          the opponents' Ace.
          Clubs: One - you can try to establish an additional trick by leading from
          the dummy toward your King.

EX. #4   Diamonds will provide all three of the additional tricks. Neither Hearts nor
          Clubs will provide more than one additional trick and both are dependent on
          a favorable lie of the opponents' cards.
          Win the first trick with the Ace of Hearts and lead the Queen of Diamonds
          to drive out the opponents' Ace. When you next win a trick, you will have
          nine sure tricks: 4 Spade tricks, 2 Heart tricks and 3 Diamond tricks.
          When taking your sure tricks in Spades, be careful to lead the King first
          and then use the Eight to go over to the Ace, Queen and Jack. Take tricks
          in the short hand first.

HAND #37 East, One Diamond; One Spade; One No Trump; Three No Trump, Three No
          Trump; South, Jack of Clubs (top of touching high cards); Nine.
          Declarer can build three extra tricks in the Spade suit if South holds the
          King. This is accompished by leading from declarer's hand toward the dummy
          and finessing dummy's Ten, hoping that North cannot win the trick with the
          King. This can be repeated twice more: leading toward dummy and finessing
          the Jack and later leading toward dummy and finessing the Queen.
          Declarer could hope to build an extra trick in the Heart suit from length.
          If each opponent has three Hearts, declarer's fourth Heart can be
          established as a trick by playing the suit three times.

Declarer can hope to establish a trick in the Diamond suit in the same fashion, by playing the suit three times. If the opponents' Diamonds are divided three and two, this will work.

Declarer cannot get more than one trick in the Club suit since the opponents have the Ace.

The Spade suit offers the best opportunity to make the contract. Declarer should win the (second) Club trick and immediately take a Spade finesse. When this is successful, he should come back to his hand, using the Ace of Diamonds and take another Spade finesse. Then he should come back to his hand with the Ace of Hearts and take a final Spade finesse.

Declarer should end up with ten tricks: 4 Spades tricks; 2 Heart tricks; 2 Diamond tricks; 1 Club trick. Declarer should not take his sure tricks in Hearts and Diamonds first because he needs his Aces as entries to his hand to allow him to take the finesses in Spades.

HAND #38   South, One Club; One Spade; Two Spades; Four Spades, Four Spades; East, King of Clubs (top of touching high cards); Ten; Eight.

Declarer can only get an extra Spade trick by ruffing a loser in dummy. Since he has three Hearts and dummy has only two, declarer can trump the third Heart in dummy and get an extra trick.

Declarer can get an extra Heart trick by leading toward the King in dummy, hoping to "trap" East's Ace.

Declarer won't be able to build extra tricks in the Diamond suit or the Club suit.

Since declarer needs two extra tricks to make the contract, he should plan to lead toward the King of Hearts to get one extra trick and then trump his third Heart with one of dummy's Spades for the second extra trick.

Declarer should take ten tricks: 6 Spade tricks (including trumping the Heart in dummy); 1 Heart trick (by leading toward the King); 2 Diamond tricks; 1 Club trick. The two techniques declarer uses with the Heart suit are "leading toward high cards" and "trumping losers."

UNIT TWENTY-SIX

EX. #1   King; Six (or Three); Queen; Jack; Three.

EX. #2   King; Ace; Six; Five (or Two); Jack.

EX. #3   Three (second hand low); King (Cover an honor with an honor); Three (Do not cover the first of touching honors.).

HAND #39   One No Trump; Three No Trump; Pass, Three No Trump.

West should choose his longest suit, Spades, and should lead a low Spade (traditionally, the fourth best, the Seven) because he does not have touching high cards.

East should play the Queen, "third hand high."

If East is allowed to win the Queen (declarer "holds up" with the Ace), he should lead back the Nine of Spades. East should return his partner's suit unless he clearly has something better to do.

West should lead another Spade. Any Spade will do, since declarer only has the Ace left. This will establish West's remaining Spades as potential tricks.

Declarer has 1 Spade trick, 2 Heart tricks and 3 Club tricks. The Diamond suit offers the best opportunity for declarer to establish the extra tricks he needs. He should plan to drive out the opponents' Ace of Diamonds and establish three extra Diamond tricks.

Declarer should not make the contract. Because West has the Diamond Ace, he will be able to win a Diamond trick and take his Spade tricks, giving the defense five tricks in total: 4 Spade tricks and 1 Diamond trick. Declarer could not make the contract against correct defense. It does not matter whether he wins the first, second or third Diamond trick if West has an entry with the Ace of Diamonds.

If East held the Ace of Diamonds, declarer could make the contract, provided he did not win the first trick with the Ace of Spades but waited until East had no Spades left.

HAND #40   One Diamond; One Heart; One No Trump; Three No Trump; Three No Trump.
North would make the opening lead. He should lead his longest suit, Spades. With no touching high cards, he should lead low, the Three. South should win the first trick with the Ace, playing "third hand high." He should then lead back the Ten of Spades. He should return his partner's suit. With only two cards left, he should lead the top of his doubleton.

After taking four Spade tricks, North should lead the Jack of Clubs, top of touching high cards.

Declarer has no tricks in Spades, four sure tricks in Hearts, one sure trick in Diamonds and two sure tricks in Clubs. The Diamond suit offers the best possibility to establish the two extra tricks declarer needs to make his contract.

If declarer leads the Jack of Diamonds (planning to take a finesse), South should play the King, following the principle of "Cover an honor with an honor."

Declarer should end up with only eight tricks: 4 Heart tricks, 2 Diamond tricks and 2 Club tricks. He cannot make the contract against best defense because he cannot avoid losing a Diamond trick in addition to the four Spade tricks.

If South does not cover the Jack of Diamonds when it is led, declarer would make the contract. He would take a finesse, playing low from his hand, and then lead another Diamond from dummy and finesse the Queen. This would allow him to take three Diamond tricks and make the contract.

If declarer plays four Heart tricks before leading Diamonds, both defenders should be careful not to discard any Diamonds. Instead they should discard Clubs. They should know to hold onto their Diamonds because West opened the bidding One Diamond and, therefore, must have at least four of them and be planning to try to establish tricks in Diamonds.

APPENDIX IV - COMPLETED SUMMARIES

OPENER'S FIRST BID

HAND VALUE

HIGH CARD POINTS		LENGTH POINTS	
Ace	4 Points	5-Card Suit	1 Point
King	3 Points	6-Card Suit	2 Points
Queen	2 Points	7-Card Suit	3 Points
Jack	1 Point	8-Card Suit	4 Points

OPENING THE BIDDING AT THE ONE-LEVEL

With less than 13 points, Pass.

With 13 to 21 points:

- Open the bidding One No Trump when you have 16 - 18 points and a balanced hand.
- Otherwise, open the bidding at the one-level in your longest suit.

If you have a choice of suits:

- Bid the higher-ranking of two five-card (or six-card) suits.
- Bid the lower-ranking of two four-card suits.
- Bid the middle-ranking of three four-card suits.

TWO NO TRUMP OPENING BID

To open the bidding Two No Trump you need a balanced hand and 22, 23 or 24 points.

THREE NO TRUMP OPENING BID

To open the bidding Three No Trump you need a balanced hand and 25, 26 or 27 points.

OPENING THE BIDDING TWO OF A SUIT

With an unbalanced hand of 22 or more points, open the bidding at the two-level in your longest suit.

- Bid the higher-ranking of two five-card (or six-card) suits.
- Bid the middle-ranking of three four-card suits.

PRE-EMPTIVE OPENING BIDS

A good suit: At least 3 of the 5 highest cards in the suit

A long suit: At least a 7-card suit

- With a 7-card suit, open at the three-level.
- With an 8-card suit, open at the four-level.
- With a 9-card suit or longer, open at the Game-level.

A weak hand: 9 - 12 points

RESPONDER'S FIRST BID

DUMMY POINTS

HIGH CARD POINTS		SHORT SUIT POINTS	
Ace	4 Points	Void	5 Points
King	3 Points	Singleton	3 Points
Queen	2 Points	Doubleton	1 Point
Jack	1 Point		

RESPONDER'S FOUR QUESTIONS

1. CAN I RAISE PARTNER'S MAJOR?
2. DO I HAVE A WEAK HAND (0 - 5 POINTS)?
3. CAN I BID A NEW SUIT AT THE ONE-LEVEL?
4. DO I HAVE A MINIMUM HAND (6 - 10 POINTS)?

RESPONSES TO AN OPENING ONE NO TRUMP BID

With 0 - 7 points:

- Bid Two Diamonds or Two Hearts or Two Spades with a 5-card suit or longer.
- Otherwise, Pass.

With 8 - 9 points:

- Bid Two No Trump with no Major Suit Fit.
- (Otherwise, Two Clubs*.)

With 10 - 14 points:

- Bid Four Hearts or Four Spades with a 6-card suit.
- Bid Three Hearts or Three Spades with a 5-card suit.
- (Bid Two Clubs with a 4-card Major suit*.)
- Otherwise, bid Three No Trump.

* Stayman Convention

RESPONSES TO AN OPENING TWO NO TRUMP BID

With 0 - 2 points, Pass.

With 3 - 8 points:

- Bid Four Hearts or Four Spades with a 6-card suit.
- Bid Three Hearts or Three Spades with a 5-card suit.
- Bid Three Clubs (Stayman) with a 4-card Major suit.
- Otherwise, bid Three No Trump.

RESPONSES AFTER AN OPENING TWO-BID

1. CAN I SUPPORT PARTNER'S MAJOR?
2. DO I HAVE A WEAK HAND (0 - 5 POINTS)?

RESPONDING TO A THREE-LEVEL PRE-EMPT

With 0 - 15 points, Pass.

With 16 or more points:

- Raise partner's Major to Game.
- Bid Four Hearts or Four Spades with a 7-card suit.
- Bid Three Hearts or Three Spades with a 5-card or 6-card suit.
- Otherwise, bid Three No Trump.

OPENER'S REBID

OPENER'S FOUR QUESTIONS

1. CAN I RAISE PARTNER'S MAJOR?
   If YES: Revalue your hand using dummy points and
   raise to the appropriate level.
   - 13 - 16 points: Raise to the two-level.
   - 17 - 18 points: Raise to the three-level.
   - 19 - 21 points: Raise to the four-level.
2. CAN I BID A NEW SUIT AT THE ONE-LEVEL?
   If YES: Bid the new suit at the appropriate level.
   - 13 - 18 points: Bid at the one-level.
   - 19 - 21 points: Bid at the two-level.
3. IS MY HAND BALANCED?
   If YES: Rebid No Trump at the appropriate level.
   - 13 - 15 points: Stay at the same level.
   - 19 - 21 points: Jump a level.
4. SHOULD I BID A NEW SUIT AT THE TWO LEVEL?
   If YES: Bid the new suit at the appropriate level.
   - 13 - 16 points: Bid your second suit. *
   - 17 - 18 points: Bid your second suit.
   - 19 - 21 points: Jump in your second suit.
   If NO: Rebid your first suit at the appropriate level
   or raise partner's Minor.
   - 13 - 16 points: Bid without jumping.
   - 17 - 18 points: Bid with a jump.
   - 19 - 21 points: Bid your suit at the four-
     level or raise partner's
     Minor to Game.

* Only if it is lower-ranking than your first suit.

OPENER'S REBID AFTER A RAISE

. After Single Raise:
   - 13 - 16 points: Pass.
   - 17 - 18 points: Raise to the three-level.
   - 19 - 21 points: Raise to the Game level.
. After Jump Raise:
   - 13 - 14 points: Pass.
   - 15 - 21 points: Raise to the Game level.
. After Game Raise:
   - 13 - 16 points: Pass.
   - 17 - 18 points: Raise to the next level.
   - 19 - 21 points: Raise to the six-level in your
     agreed trump suit.

OPENER'S REBID AFTER A
TWO-CLUB (STAYMAN) RESPONSE

. Two Hearts: 4-card (or longer) Heart suit
. Two Spades: 4-card (or longer) Spade suit
. Two Diamonds: No 4-card Major

RESPONDER'S REBID

HOW HIGH

THE KEY QUESTION FOR DECIDING HOW HIGH

Do we have 26 combined points?
If the answer is YES: Play in a Game contract.
If the answer is NO: Play in a Part-Game contract.

WHERE

THE KEY QUESTION FOR DECIDING WHERE
WHEN BIDDING TO A GAME CONTRACT

Do we have a Magic Major Suit Fit?
If the answer is YES: Play in Four Hearts or Four Spades.
If the answer is NO: Play in Three No Trump.

THE KEY QUESTION FOR DECIDING WHERE
WHEN BIDDING TO A PART-GAME CONTRACT

Do we have any Magic Fit?
If the answer is YES: Play Part-Game in that suit.
If the answer is NO: Play Part-Game in No Trump.

RESPONDER'S REBID WHEN OPENER
COULD HAVE A MINIMUM HAND

Ask yourself HOW HIGH and WHERE.
   With 6 - 10 points, Game is unlikely so make a
   discouraging rebid:
   - Pass.
   - Bid an old suit at the two-level.
   - Bid One No Trump.
   With 11 - 12 points, Game is likely so make an
   encouraging rebid:
   - Bid an old suit at the three-level.
   - Bid Two No Trump.
   With 13 or more points, Game is certain so make
   sure you get there:
   - Bid Game if you know WHERE.
   - Bid a new suit if you don't know WHERE.

RESPONDER'S REBID WHEN OPENER
SHOWS A MEDIUM HAND

With 6 - 8 points: Choose the best Part-Game.
With 9 or more points: Bid Game or make a marathon bid.

RESPONDER'S REBID WHEN OPENER
SHOWS A MAXIMUM HAND

With 6 or more points: Bid Game or make a descriptive bid.
The bidding must continue until Game is reached.

COMPETITIVE ACTIONS

REQUIREMENTS FOR MAKING AN OVERCALL

- A 5-card suit or longer
- An opening bid (13 - 21 points)

REQUIREMENTS FOR A ONE NO TRUMP OVERCALL

- 16 - 18 points
- Balanced hand

REQUIREMENTS FOR A TAKE-OUT DOUBLE

- Support for the unbid suits
- 13 - 21 dummy points

PENALTY OR TAKE-OUT?

A Double is for Take-out if neither you nor your partner has bid and you are doubling a Part-Game contract.
A Double is for Penalty if either you or your partner has bid or you are doubling a Game contract or higher.

PRE-EMPTIVE JUMP OVERCALLS

A good suit: At least 3 of the 5 highest cards in the suit
A long suit: At least a 6-card suit

- With a 6-card suit, jump to the two-level.
- With a 7-card suit, jump to the three-level.
- With an 8-card suit, jump to the four-level.
- With a 9-card suit or longer, jump to the Game-level.

A weak hand: 9 - 12 points (not enough to overcall)

BIDDING OVER AN OPPONENT'S PRE-EMPT

With 0 - 15 points, Pass.
With 16 - 21 points:

- Overcall with a 5-card suit or longer.
- Double with support for the unbid suits.
- Overcall Three No Trump.

With 22 or more points, Cue Bid the opponent's suit.

RESPONDING IN COMPETITION

RESPONDING TO AN OVERCALL

1. CAN I RAISE PARTNER'S MAJOR?
   If YES: Revalue your hand using dummy points and
   raise to the appropriate level.

0 - 5 points:	Pass.
6 - 10 points:	Raise to the two-level.
11 - 12 points:	Raise to the three-level.
13 - 16 points:	Raise to the four-level.

2. DO I HAVE A WEAK HAND (0 - 5 POINTS)?
   If YES: Pass.
3. CAN I BID A NEW SUIT AT THE ONE-LEVEL?
   If YES: Bid the appropriate suit.
4. DO I HAVE A MINIMUM HAND (6 - 10 POINTS)?
   If YES: Raise opener's Minor suit to the two-level.
   Bid One No Trump.
   If NO: Raise opener's Minor suit to the three-level
   with 11 - 12 points.
   Raise opener's Minor suit to Game with
   13 - 16 points and 3-card support.
   Bid a new suit at the two-level.

RESPONDING TO A TAKE-OUT DOUBLE

With 0 - 10 points:

- Bid a 4-card or longer unbid Major suit at the cheapest available level.
- Bid a 4-card or longer unbid Minor suit at the cheapest available level.
- Bid One No Trump (rare response).

With 11 - 12 points:

- Jump in a 4-card or longer unbid Major suit.
- Jump in a 4-card or longer unbid Minor suit.
- Jump to Two No Trump (rare response).

With 13 or more points:

- Bid Game in a 4-card or longer unbid Major suit.
- Jump to Three No Trump.

COMPETITIVE AUCTIONS

When responding to partner's opening bid or overcall, continue to use Responder's Four Questions even if your right-hand opponent interferes.
If an opponent's bid interferes with your normal response, find a suitable substitute. With 6 - 10 points, Pass with no suitable bid. With 11 or more points, bid something.
When an opponent bids after your partner has made a take-out Double:

0 - 5 points:	Pass.
6 - 10 points:	Bid an unbid suit or One No Trump
11 - 12 points:	Jump in an unbid suit or bid Two No Trump.
13 - 16 points:	Bid Game.

When an opponent makes a take-out Double of partner's opening bid, respond as if the opponent had said Pass.

DEFENDER'S PLAY

CHOOSING THE SUIT TO LEAD AGAINST NO TRUMP

If partner has bid a suit, lead that suit.
Otherwise, lead your longest suit.
With two equally long suits, lead the stronger suit.

CHOOSING THE LEAD AGAINST A TRUMP CONTRACT

If partner has bid a suit, lead that suit.
Otherwise:
- Lead a suit in which you have touching high cards.
- Lead a short suit (other than the trump suit).
- Lead an unbid suit.

LEADING PARTNER'S SUIT

Lead the top of a doubleton (A 2, K 3).
Lead the top of touching high cards (Q J 7, K J 10).
Lead low from three or more cards when you lack
touching high cards (Q 9 3, K J 5, Q 7 6 4, 7 6 3).

LEADING YOUR SUIT

Lead the top of touching high cards (K Q J 3, A K 7).
Otherwise, lead low (K J 8 4 3, Q 9 7 2).

DEFENSIVE GUIDELINES

- Second player to a trick plays low.
- Third player to a trick plays high.
- Cover an honor with an honor.

GAME CONTRACTS

Game in No Trump: Three No Trump
Game in a Major Suit: Four Hearts or Four Spades
Game in a Minor Suit: Five Clubs or Five Diamonds

BIDDING MESSAGES

Sign-off: Partner must pass.
Invitational: Partner may bid or pass.
Forcing: Partner must bid again.
Marathon: The partnership keeps bidding until game
              at least is reached.

DECLARER PLAY

DECLARER'S FOUR QUESTIONS

1. HOW MANY TRICKS DO I NEED?
   - Add six to the level of your contract.
2. HOW MANY SURE TRICKS DO I HAVE?
   - Add together the number of sure tricks in each suit.
3. HOW CAN I BUILD EXTRA TRICKS?
   - By promoting high cards
   - By length
   - By leading toward high cards
   - By trumping losers (if playing in a trump contract)
4. HOW DO I PUT IT ALL TOGETHER?
   - Choose from among your alternatives the safest and
     surest way of building the extra tricks needed to
     fulfill your contract.

GUIDELINES FOR PLAYING NO TRUMP CONTRACTS

- Take your tricks when you have enough to make your
  contract.
- Build the tricks you need for your contract before taking
  your sure tricks.
- Find the longest combined suit and play it first.
- Watch your entries to be sure that you can get to the hand
  from which you want to lead to the next trick.

GUIDELINES FOR PLAYING SUIT CONTRACTS

- Check to see if you need to trump a loser in dummy before
  drawing trumps.
- Draw trumps until the opponents have no more.
- Build the tricks you need for your contract before taking
  your sure tricks.
- Do not make a special effort to trump tricks in your hand.

THE SLAM DECISIONS

HOW HIGH: 33 or more combined points are needed
           for a Small Slam.
           37 or more combined points are needed
           for a Grand Slam.
WHERE: Play Slam in any Magic Fit, otherwise
           in No Trump.